Beyond Java™

Bruce A. Tate

O'REILLY®

Beijing · Cambridge · Farnham · Köln · Paris · Sebastopol · Taipei · Tokyo

Beyond Java™
by Bruce A. Tate

Copyright © 2005 O'Reilly Media, Inc. All rights reserved.
Printed in the United States of America.

Published by O'Reilly Media, Inc., 1005 Gravenstein Highway North, Sebastopol, CA 95472.

O'Reilly books may be purchased for educational, business, or sales promotional use. Online editions are also available for most titles (*safari.oreilly.com*). For more information, contact our corporate/institutional sales department: (800) 998-9938 or *corporate@oreilly.com*.

Editor:	Michael Loukides
Production Editor:	Darren Kelly
Cover Designer:	Ellie Volckhausen
Interior Designer:	David Futato

Printing History:

September 2005:   First Edition.

 This book uses RepKover™, a durable and flexible lay-flat binding.

ISBN: 0-596-10094-9

[M]

Table of Contents

Preface

In March of 2005, I was shocked and honored to get the word that one of my books, *Better, Faster, Lighter Java* (O'Reilly), won a Jolt award for technical excellence. I talked about how Java™ developers could buck standing conventions to build better applications, faster than before. That book will always have a special place in my heart. Yet, throughout the process, something was in the way, and I couldn't quite put my finger on it.

Around this time, one of my customers was building an application consisting of a complex database schema with a web-based user interface. We'd been using Spring and Hibernate with Web Work, a common stack for lightweight Java development, and we'd been generally pleased. Some things bugged us, though: the amount of repetition, the proliferation of XML configuration, and the pace of our changes. On a whim, we tried Ruby on Rails, a surprisingly productive and innovative framework that's sweeping quickly through non-Java communities, and is making some noise among Java architects, too. We were shocked with our productivity, and we moved the project to the new foundation.

Something clicked into place for me. For this kind of application, Java itself was in the way. Remove it from the equation, and I could reduce the amount of code by a factor of four, drive the XML down to one-tenth of what it was, and achieve stunning productivity, with good performance. Better still, the concepts in *Better, Faster, Lighter Java* still applied. For other projects, if I needed the community and tools that Java offered, I could use it instead. If I didn't need Java, I could take the principles in *BFLJ* to the extreme. A dam inside me broke, and this new book started pouring out. I had a message.

Months later, I found an audience, thousands of miles and 19 hours from home. I fidgeted nervously before the Java User's Group. I'd certainly addressed larger groups, but this trip was different. In this case, the Norwegian Java User's Group had paid my travel expenses to Oslo, not to sing the praises of Spring, or Hibernate, or agile development, but to call their baby ugly. It was hard for me. After writing the bestsellers, getting the Jolt, and building a thriving consulting practice in a down economy, I wanted the Java train to roll on, unstoppable, always building on an ever-strengthening foundation. I wanted Java to send my productivity through the roof, and for the impressive community and brain power to solve all the tough problems that Java faces today, but nothing lasts forever.

In the talk, I didn't pick an eventual winner. I laid out the reasons for Java's success, and then talked through its most serious problems. I showed some alternative languages and frameworks, as I saw them. Throughout the talk, I pointed out that conditions are ripe for an alternative to emerge. As I addressed the hospitable group, I answered questions and read faces. A few looked hostile, or hurt. Most others showed understanding, and a little fear. They understood my central thrust. For many of the most common problems that we solve with Java, some other frameworks in other languages can already do a better job. In some cases, the productivity discrepancy is wide enough to merit a serious look.

The talk, and the questions, went on way too long, but nobody left. They were surprisingly receptive. After the presentation, we went out to see some of Oslo. One of the hostile attendees cornered me for most of the night. The hard questions just wouldn't quit coming:

- Why can't we improve Java to cover the shortcomings?
- Do the other frameworks and languages that you presented have enough commercial backing?
- What about distributed transactions, or web services, or XML support?
- How can you find programmers, or train the ones you find?

These questions are real, and they show the tremendous barriers of entry against emerging languages. My questioner was a gentleman, but he could not completely hide his agitation or his deep-seated belief that the hurdles for the next successful language are incredibly high, and that we'll still be coding in Java for the foreseeable future. He could well be right. But I've come to recognize some real limitations in the Java language, and many of the frameworks that power it. For certain problems, Java just isn't productive enough for me anymore. I've experienced success with some alternatives. Though a language can last half a century to support legacy applications, I know no language can keep its leadership and its luster forever. Java's reign will end. It's not a question of *if*, but *when*.

Who Should Read This Book?

When C++ faded into relative obscurity, many of my best friends got burned, badly. They didn't recognize that change was in the air, or how violently change could come. Though I have a whole lot to lose, I'm writing this book because I don't want to see it happen again. If you don't want to be caught by surprise, you need to read this book.

If you think I'm right, you can start to build your skills accordingly. You might download some of the frameworks I discuss, and learn a few new languages. This book will teach you what a new language needs to succeed. If I've gotten lucky and found one of the likely winners, you'll be just a little bit more prepared when things do change.

If you think I am wrong, you can use the best techniques from the best frameworks written in any language to improve what you're doing in Java today. New frameworks like PHP, C Omega for .NET, and Ruby on Rails will come occasionally. You need to know about them, and understand how to evaluate them.

Either way, you win. It's time to start paying attention again. It's time to look to the horizon, beyond Java.

Conventions

The following typographical conventions are used in this book:

Italic

> Used for filenames, directories, emphasis, and first use of a technical term.

`Constant width`

> Used in code examples and for class names, method names, and objects.

`Constant width italic`

> Indicates an item that should be replaced with an actual value in your program.

`Constant width bold`

> Used for user input in text and in examples showing both input and output. Also used for emphasis in code, and in order to indicate a block of text included in an annotated call-out.

Using Code Examples

This book is here to help you get your job done. In general, you may use the code in this book in your programs and documentation. You do not need to contact O'Reilly for permission unless you're reproducing a significant portion of the code. For example, writing a program that uses several chunks of code from this book does not require permission. Selling or distributing a CD-ROM of examples from O'Reilly books *does* require permission. Answering a question by citing this book and quoting example code does not require permission. Incorporating a significant amount of example code from this book into your product's documentation *does* require permission.

We appreciate, but do not require, attribution. An attribution usually includes the title, author, publisher, and ISBN. For example: "*Beyond Java* by Bruce A. Tate. Copyright 2005 O'Reilly Media, Inc., 0-596-10094-9."

If you feel your use of code examples falls outside fair use or the permission given above, feel free to contact us at *permissions@oreilly.com*.

Comments and Questions

Please address comments and questions concerning this book to the publisher:

> O'Reilly Media, Inc.
> 1005 Gravenstein Highway North
> Sebastopol, CA 95472
> (800) 998-9938 (in the United States or Canada)
> (707) 829-0515 (international/local)
> (707) 829-0104 (fax)

There is a web page for this book, which lists errata, examples, or any additional information. You can access this page at:

> *http://www.oreilly.com/catalog/beyondjava*

To comment or ask technical questions about this book, send email to:

> *bookquestions@oreilly.com*

For information about books, conferences, Resource Centers, and the O'Reilly Network, see the O'Reilly web site at:

> *http://www.oreilly.com*

Safari® Enabled

 When you see a Safari® Enabled icon on the cover of your favorite technology book, it means the book is available online through the O'Reilly Network Safari Bookshelf.

Safari offers a solution that's better than e-books. It's a virtual library that lets you easily search thousands of top technology books, cut and paste code samples, download chapters, and find quick answers when you need the most accurate, current information. Try it for free at *http://safari.oreilly.com*.

Acknowledgments

This book challenged me more than any other book I've written. I felt that I needed to bolster my opinions with those of other respected programmers and consultants. I asked for many opinions, and published some of the responses. Thanks to Mike Clark, Matt Raible, Andrew Hunt, Ramnivas Laddad, Brett McLaughlin, and Eitan Suez for answering my questions. Thanks especially to Glenn Vanderburg, Ted Neward, Erik Hatcher, Justin Gehtland, James Duncan Davidson, Jim Weirich, Jamis Buck, David Heinemeier Hansson, Dion Almaer, Jason Hunter, Richard Monson-Haefel, Stuart Halloway, and Dennis Sosnoski for agreeing to let me post your interviews in the book. Thanks again to Justin Gehtland for use of your metrics, and being a partner through two writing projects.

Special thanks go to David Heinemeier Hansson for access to your framework and community from the inside. When I needed reviewers, you used your influence to find them for me. When I had hard questions, you answered them. You also provide the irresistible force that is Ruby on Rails. I'm grateful. I hope this book marks only the beginning of a partnership, and a possible friendship.

Dave Thomas, you have given me the courage and faith to explore things beyond Java. You've been a role model for me. Your consistent honor and class teach me; your skill with your keyboard and your voice inspire me; your business sense instructs me. Avi Bryant, thanks for your tireless work and promotion on the Seaside framework.

Special thanks also go out to Michael Loukides. Supporting me is your job, but I also feel a special kinship. We've been through a lot together, and I aim for that relationship to continue. You've been very good for me and my writing career. I hope you've benefited in some small way, too.

After letting my readers down by publishing *Spring, A Developer's Notebook* before it was ready, I feel the need to offer some thanks for helping me through the negative press. O'Reilly, you were great to stand behind me. I felt that I needed to have this book reviewed exhaustively, to prevent the same mistake from happening twice. Many answered the call. Ted Neward, Venkat Subramaniam, Michael Koziarski, Jeremy Kemper, Michael Loukides (who gave me advice and ideas far beyond the usual editorial support), and many others too numerous to list here provided good reviews.

Invariably, some reviewers take on a book as a personal mission. Usually, a book is lucky to have one such reviewer. This time, I had four. Steve Yegge, Jason Hunter, David Rupp, and Curt Hibbs all went far beyond the call of duty. They provided help that was stylistic, philosophical, technical, and even structural. This book is radically different from my initial vision. Thanks to all who contributed.

To Jay Zimmerman and all of those I've met at NoFluffJustStuff, this book is as much yours as it is mine. You've helped me shape and sharpen these ideas, and you've given me a platform to present them.

Most of all, I've got to recognize the contributions of one special lady in my life. She propped me up when I was too low to write, she talked through many of the ideas, she sat through many boring dinners as I talked through this stuff with anyone who would listen. Her smile fills my soul with the passion that I need for writing, and gives me a reason to be. We share a common purpose in raising our daughters, Kayla and Julia, a common foundation of faith in Jesus Christ, an unending hospitality for weary colleagues on the road, and a sense of adventure in life. Without you, I'm nothing. With you, I feel like I matter, and my ideas matter. You're a bigger part of this book than you'll ever know. I love you always.

CHAPTER 1

Owls and Ostriches

Some kayakers that I know have a death wish. They bomb down Class V runs with reckless abandon. It seems like a matter of time before they run that waterfall that has trapped deadwood underneath it. Such an obstacle would trap the boat, and the force of the river would pin the boater underwater. They're like ostriches, ignoring the danger with their head in the sand.

There's another kind of boater, though. When I first started kayaking, I scouted everything. I would stop at the most casual Class II+ (beginner) ripple to look it over and set up safety ropes for 45 minutes before making the run. Often, I'd run out of time on a river, and be forced to bomb down a bottom section to complete it before nightfall. Now, I rarely get out of my boat to scout most minor rapids. In certain places, it's just not practical. Instead, I use chase boating techniques, invented in the narrow, steep rivers of the Southeast, to improve my chances. I don't boat this way because I like danger. In fact, I've honed my instincts to understand where danger is most likely to be. I boat this way because it lets me focus my scouting time where I need it most. These boaters are the owls.

It comes down to this. I'll often ignore risks involving minor consequences or low frequencies because dealing with the risk is not wise. Managing the risks properly may take too much effort, money, or time, opening me up to additional risk, which brings me back to owls and ostriches. Normally, there's a huge difference between the two, but occasionally, owls will get overconfident or make minor errors in risk assessment, and convince themselves to run something dangerous without scouting. That's happened to me. I've run the same creek hundreds of times, and something changes like higher river levels or the creek bed after a flood. There's a fine line between owls and ostriches. Sometimes, it's even tough to tell the difference between the two. As a kayaker, even if I've decided to ignore certain kinds of risks on certain rivers and conditions, I've sometimes got to step back and reassess the risk. That's the subject of this book.

Ignorance as a Virtue

In many ways, kayaking is like programming. I've learned an incredible trick. I can be surprisingly productive by simply ignoring most problems. With a little luck, the problems often just go away. Such an attitude can work for you or against you. Many post office clerks and minimum-wage fast food employees have learned that the same technique actually works for their problems, also known as customers. These are ostriches. If you look closely, you can find some selective, wise application of ignorance—the owl's trademark. I actually find that most "problems" in programming are merely *potential* problems. If you've read any of my books, you know that I preach against the dangers of premature optimization, and echo the popular agile principle of *YAGNI*: "You ain't gonna need it." I usually ignore bloated frameworks that promise to save me time, trusting my instincts to simpler solutions.

More to the point, I've found that Java does everything that I need, so I haven't looked beyond these borders for a very long time. Ignorance is bliss. I know some languages are more dynamic, and possibly more productive in spurts, but in the end, it seems like Java will always win. It's got tens of thousands of frameworks to do anything from running systems for nuclear reactors to programming an embedded controller on a power toenail clipper. Many of the best frameworks are even free. I can always find a Java developer to do what I need. I know that people have made it work to solve massive problems. And I know that my customers will feel safe and secure. In short, the community and breadth of Java have always trumped anything that the alternatives have to offer. So I quit looking. And I'm glad that I did, because it allowed me to focus on building a consulting business and satisfying my customers instead of doing exhausting research for every new problem.

When a dominant language or technology is in its prime, there's a blissful ignorance stage, when ignoring alternatives works in your favor. Figure 1-1 shows what I mean. When a new language arrives with the power and dominance of a Java or C++, you can afford to ignore alternatives for a while. But if you don't accurately identify the end of the cycle, you can get steamrolled. Suddenly, your competition has the jump on you, with much better productivity leading to better quality, improved productivity, and more customers. When you enter the transition time, you'd better start paying attention.

I admit unashamedly that I liked having my head in the sand. It was easy, and productive, and politically safe. I bet that many of you Java developers act like me. You may have your own reasons. Living in this shelter is certainly easier—doing nothing trumps extra work. You might feel safer—no one ever got fired for choosing IBM. (OK, so maybe Component Broker on

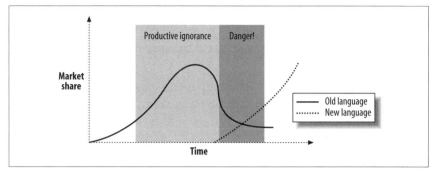

Figure 1-1. For a period of time, ignorance is productive, but the ending of that period can be unpredictable

OS/2 was not such a good idea....) You may have an incredible investment in skills that you believe will not commute, and if you've invested poorly in your skill set, you may be right. You may be bound like a Siamese twin to Java by a long-term project or a group based on the language. Like my reasons, many of these are sound.

Shaken to the Core

After living in blissful ignorance for five years or more, I had an experience that shook me to the core. I led a new start-up down a path that required what I'd consider three of the most productive lightweight frameworks out there for web development of persistence applications: Hibernate, Spring, and Web Work. I knew there were slightly more productive environments for this kind of thing, but they either would not scale (in terms of complexity or performance), or were not popular enough to justify the risk.

My partner and I decided to implement a small part of the application in Ruby on Rails, a highly productive web-based programming framework. We did this not to satisfy our customer, but to satisfy a little intellectual curiosity. The results astounded us:

- For the rewrite, we programmed faster. Much faster. It took Justin, my lead programmer, four nights to build what it had taken four months to build in Java. We estimated that we were between 5 and 10 times more productive.
- We generated one-fourth the lines of code; one-fifth if you consider configuration files.
- The productivity gains held up after we moved beyond the rewrite.
- The Ruby on Rails version of the application performed faster. This is probably not true of all possible use cases, but for our application, the

RoR active record persistence strategy trumped Hibernate's Object Relational Mapping (ORM), at least with minimal tuning.

- The customer cared much more about productivity than being on a safe Java foundation.

As you can well imagine, this shook my world view down to the foundation. I'm now frantically trying to catch up. It seems that conditions on the river changed without my noticing. I've got to start scouting again.

Boiling Frogs

Let's look at it still another way. You've doubtlessly heard that if you put a frog in hot water, it will leap out, but if you slowly bring tepid water to a boil, the frog will die contentedly. And of course, that's the debate that I hope to trigger in this book. Are the waters around us warming? Notice at the end of my introduction, the owl and the ostrich are exactly the same when it comes to consequences. They may not recognize it, but motivations don't matter one little bit. If the water starts to boil, if the conditions on the river change, they'll both die.

This past year, I decided to wake up to my surroundings to test the water around me. I learned both Ruby and aspect-oriented programming (AOP). After checking the temperature, I think the water is actually heating up. It's not boiling yet, and I don't know if it will ever boil. But I do know that I'm going to keep a close eye on the temperature for a while, and I hope to convince you to do the same. Let me tell you why.

Danger Signs

A large number of the applications that we write put a web-based frontend over a database, sometimes with additional business rules and sometimes without. Yet, after more than five years of solving this problem over and over, we still can't solve it very quickly in the Java space. Further, most Java framework developers are making incremental changes that won't truly revolutionize web development. Building a new team to solve this problem in the right way is a demanding job. Building a team from, say, COBOL programmers, is nearly impossible. The language is too alien, the frameworks too extensive, and the landscape too unstable. Even with seasoned developers, it takes a surprising amount of code to get even simple applications off the ground.

Jason Hunter: The Next Big Thing
Author of *Java Servlet Programming*

Jason Hunter works as a lead applications engineer at Mark Logic. He's the author of Java Servlet Programming *(O'Reilly). As Apache's representative to the Java Community Process Executive Committee, he established a landmark agreement allowing open source Java. He is publisher of Servlets.com and XQuery.com, is an original contributor to Apache Tomcat, is a member of the expert groups responsible for Servlet, JSP, JAXP, and XQJ API development, and has participated in the W3C XQuery Working Group. He also co-created the open source JDOM library to enable optimized Java and XML integration.*

Is Java in danger of losing its leadership position?

JH: Java's already ended its leadership run. It happened maybe two years ago when the best brains in the industry stopped focusing on Java as a technology and started splitting off into other areas of interest. It's only gotten worse as of late. The departure of Josh Bloch and Neal Gaftner to Google is a high-profile sign of the changing tide. But they're not alone. If you want to push the envelope these days, you don't do it by innovating on Java. You may do it with Java, but not on Java.

It doesn't mean Java's dead. It just means Java isn't cutting edge anymore. It's plenty understood, plenty stable, and entirely ready for outsourcing.

What's next?

JH: What's next? I don't think there's one thing. There's definitely not one language. Java's still the ubiquitous language. The innovation now is happening on top. Exciting areas: web remoting (a.k.a. Ajax), search (a.k.a. Google and XQuery), and folksonomies (a.k.a. flickr tags).

I have a very practical way of evaluating what is the hot technology: [determining] what earns you the most money being a trainer of that technology. Java definitely was the hot technology for years. I earned twice what the C++ trainers were receiving. It wasn't that Java was harder, just that there was more demand than supply.

If you train on something commoditized (like C++ was and Java is now), you get mass-market rates. If you train on something too bleeding edge, you don't get enough customers.

I don't see any movement right now that's got the same huge swell potential as Java had. What are the "alpha geeks" doing, as Tim O'Reilly calls them? Well, James Davidson dug deeply into the Mac. But there's not a huge amount of room for experts in that market. There aren't enough business dollars to be earned. I've gone into XQuery, which I've found a fun and useful way to bring search ideas "in-house" and put you in control of what you find and what you do with it. Mike Clark became an expert on automation. My advice to people without a target yet is to learn Subversion and help companies transition from CVS to SVN.

But we're all going in separate ways. We've agreed on the Java base, but are diverging on what we do with that now-ubiquitous standard.

Your questions are very focused on Java and "alternatives to Java." The Web wasn't an alternative to Windows. It was different. The tech phase we're in now isn't about an alternative to Java. It's different. We're going to take Java for granted just like we take CPUs for granted: it's necessary. It was once the place where all the money was; now it's more of a commodity.

Complexity

Java seems to be moving away from its base. You might solve the hardest problems more easily, but it's much harder to create simple web apps than it ever has been before. James Duncan Davidson calls this problem *approach-ability*. When Java was young, you didn't have to know much to build a basic applet. Now, to build a simple web app using the most popular frameworks, you need to know much more.

True, open source tools are changing the productivity of Java dramatically, in the best possible ways. Tremendous tools like Hibernate and Spring can let you build enterprise-strength applications with much less effort. But it can take a whole year to confidently learn how to wield these tools with skill. AOP can also help, by letting you write plain old Java objects (POJOs) for your business rules, and isolate services in prepackaged aspects like security and transactions. These abstractions, though, make an ever-rising river for the novice to navigate. My question is this: how high is too high? I think we're already getting too high for most novices. I no longer feel comfortable telling a client that they can retrain the average COBOL programmer on Java. There's just too much to learn, and it takes too much time.

In the past, complex problems drove higher abstraction. When computers got too big for people to code with wires, experts programmed with machine code. When those programs got too big for people to understand, they organized the machine codes and data with symbols in assembler language. Rising complexity led to high-level languages, structured programming, and object-oriented programming. My contention is that this higher river of complexity will flood, forcing us to adopt a new abstraction, sooner rather than later.

Rapid revolution

There's been an incredible amount of innovation around Java in the past three years. You've experienced a transition from the heavyweight containers like EJB to lightweight containers like Spring. You've likely moved from EJB or JDBC persistence to iBATIS, JDO, or Hibernate. You're possibly seeing the wisdom of moving beyond Struts to something like Tapestry. It's been my experience that most innovation is driven by need. My theory is that revolution increases dramatically when complexity hits a certain threshold. The only evidence that I have to support this theory is circumstantial:

- The overpowering new mountains of persistence frameworks
- The proliferation of model-view-controller (MVC) frameworks
- The growth of containers
- The rapid introduction of XML-binding frameworks

I'm suggesting that inventions usually accompany a need. When we get something that's right or merely close enough, like Ant or JUnit, we leave it alone until it doesn't fit our purposes anymore.

Experienced developers likely will not understand the excruciating process of learning enough to build the simplest web application in Java. Many of them will complain that I am overstating this issue. If you're in that group, I challenge you to find a smart, inexperienced Java developer who's learning the whole stack of applications that you need to do enterprise web development, and interview him. The problem is twofold. First, it's hard. Second, the consequences for failure are dire. If you pick the wrong horse once, or get locked up for three years on a big project with dated technology, you'll be just about starting over when you move on to the next project. The implications of the churn are staggering. To me, they may mean that code needs to be happening at a higher level of abstraction, and we've been incapable of finding it in Java.

Unnatural stretching

Increasingly, you're probably stretching Java beyond its intended directions. It's just a plain fact that the object you code with plain Java is not enough anymore. I made the point in *Better, Faster, Lighter Java* that trying to code all crosscutting services and all behaviors into business objects is folly, and inheritance does not go far enough. You've got to use tricks, like compile-time byte code enhancement or runtime code generation with proxies, to make the object transparent. You are now stretching Java beyond its intended purpose, and that's good...to a point. You're also increasing the barrier to entry. Ask any novice who's tried to troubleshoot a problem with Hibernate's lazy loading, or Spring's proxies.

I've also noticed that other, more dynamic languages rarely use things like AOP or dependency injection. Those features solve critical problems in Java, but more dynamic languages like Smalltalk, Python, and Ruby don't have the same level of pain.

I'm not saying that these are bad technologies. They absolutely destroy the closest heavyweight alternatives, in terms of simplicity and power. They're solving hard problems. It's just that your mind can learn only so much, only so fast. Java's rapidly becoming an effective tool set for elite developers. Hey, maybe that's where programming is going. I'm just saying that this unnatural stretching is one more clue that it may be time to take the temperature of the water around you.

Language evolution

Java 5 is strongly touted as perhaps the most innovative major release of Java in half a decade. I do agree that it's going to have a significant impact. I'm not at all convinced that all of the impact will be positive. I regularly attend a conference called NoFluffJustStuff. The experts at the conference sit on a panel and answer questions. One of my favorite questions deals with new features in the language. The whole panel agrees that generics, as implemented, are a bad idea. That usually shocks the audience.

If you think about it, the Java generics Java Specification Request (JSR) introduces a whole lot of syntax to solve a marginal problem with no corresponding change to the Java virtual machine (JVM). I'm guessing that the typical Java developer rarely gets a class cast exception. And there are plenty of opportunities. Most of the objects in a typical Java application are usually in collections anyway. Whenever you take them out of the collection, you've got to cast them from Object anyway. At that point, type safety gives you about as much protection as a lap belt in a burning, plummeting 747. Yet, the generics syntax is invasive, and the implementation is worse. In an age when more and more experts assert that dynamic typing leads to simpler applications and productive programmers, Java developers are learning how to build stronger enforcement for static types.

Add questionable use of legitimate features like annotations, which can completely change the semantics of your program without conventional code, and you've got all kinds of possible trouble. Does the increase in power offset the increase in complexity and obscurity? Annotations bring a completely new tool, and in many ways a programming model, to the Java community. I don't know enough to say whether we'll learn to use annotations well, but I do feel comfortable predicting a few major disasters while we learn.

I don't want to tip my whole hand too early. I'll talk more about Java limitations in Chapters 3 through 5. Right now, just understand that Java is experiencing some real problems. They may be growing pains of youth, or they might be arthritis in Java's October years. I just don't know, but the temperature is rising fast enough to get my attention.

What's Good Is GOOD

I don't mean to say that Java's bugler is finishing the last few notes of "Taps" as you read this paragraph. Instead of spewing doom and gloom, I'd rather tell owls and ostriches alike to pick up your eyes, and watch and listen. Look at it like this: *conditions are ripe for a credible alternative to emerge*. At the time of printing, Java's still the king of the hill. In fact, powerful and compelling motivations still drive new investment in Java:

- The Java community is vibrant. You can find talent to attack hard problems in Java. You can also find supporting staff, like salespeople and project managers, who know Java.
- Most major commercial vendors support Java, or a close derivative (C#). As a result, you can buy applications, servers, components, tools, services, and even management consoles for Java.
- Open source is a thriving force in its own right, and it is driving incredible innovation daily.
- Academic institutions teach Java development, and do research on many Java-related problems. I recently worked with a start-up that's working on a tool, born in a university research lab, that can predict Java performance, given a UML diagram.
- The JVM is a powerful innovation in its own right, and allows unprecedented portability. Some experts believe that the JVM may be more important than the Java language itself.

Now, you might believe, as I recently did, that all of this vibrant community trumps any language advantage, in all but the most extreme problems. And even if you did find such a problem, what's the compelling alternative? How will it ever find enough developers to reach a critical mass?

You're probably thinking: face it, Bruce, there's .NET and Java, and .NET is, by design, as close as legally possible to Java. Adopting .NET would be like overhauling your diet by swearing off McDonalds, and going to Burger King every day. After that, there's nothing.

This much is true. If there is no credible alternative, your best course is to keep looking inside the Java community for answers. In that case, this is a dead book, and you can just let it be. But give me a few more pages, lest you close it too soon.

New Horizons

Keep in mind that I'm a cynic at heart. When it comes to technologies, it takes a whole lot of effort to get me excited. I still have never written a web service, at least with the massive IBM and Microsoft stacks, and I didn't write my first EJB until 2003. I've never written an EJB entity bean unless it was to build a case against them, and never will. I've instead preferred simpler architectures, like REST, POJO programming, transparent persistence, and Spring. Even then, I was late to those parties.

It's even tougher to get me to play with a new language. Dave Thomas, a highly respected programmer and a gifted teacher, is fond of saying that you should learn a new programming language every couple of months. I've probably averaged one every five years, and I rarely do more than dabble. But recently, in my dabbling, I've found a couple of startling innovations. These frameworks had ideas that just about reached out and ripped me out of my chair this year.

I've taken a little more time than usual to survey the interesting innovations around new programming languages. When it comes to building web pages and application servers, two ideas have my undivided attention: metaprogramming (like Ruby on Rails) and continuation servers (like Seaside on Smalltalk). Neither of these two innovations is happening with much impact in Java. You'll get a deeper treatment in Chapters 7 and 8, but it's enough to say for now that they are both many times more productive than their Java alternatives.

Dynamic Languages

Java is a language with many compromises. Many of the features of Java are appropriate for building operating system extensions and middleware, but limit application development. Consider this Ruby fragment:

```
something = "Owls and Ostriches"
4.times {puts something}
```

These simple little lines of code print `Owls` and `Ostriches` four times. Look at the power in this language:

- You don't have to worry about details like typing, if you don't want to. If it walks like a duck and quacks like a duck, Ruby will type it as a duck. This saves more time than you think.

- 4 is an object. Everything is an object. You can send methods to a 4, or a string, just like any other object in the system.

- `{puts something}` is a code block. You can pass a code block as a parameter, and Ruby lets methods deal with the code blocks. This construct dramatically simplifies things like iteration, and lets you quickly customize the inside of a loop in a library.

Taken by themselves, these features can make you much more productive. But add the other features of a dynamic language, and you can see incredible power and productivity very quickly. Many of the so-called scripting languages make much more sense for application developers.

Metaprogramming

The Java community is now investing enormous energy into programming styles that are more transparent, reflective, and dynamic. These approaches are called *metaprogramming*, because they spend more time in the realm of the class than the object. It makes sense that you can get more leverage that way. Transparent persistence frameworks like Hibernate teach generic classes and collections to be persistent. AOP lets you extend a specified list of methods with custom code, without requiring modifications of that method. These problems are metaprogramming problems.

When Java experts get excited about metaprogramming, they often wind up adopting other languages. Want some examples? David Geary, one of Java's most successful authors and JSF expert group member, is aggressively learning Ruby on Rails, and is writing a Rails book. James Duncan Davidson, creator of Tomcat and Ant, left the Java community to code Objective C for the Mac environment. And, as you have seen, Justin Gehtland and I are using Rails to implement a web-based application for a start-up.

Think of metaprogramming as building a high-level builder. Ruby on Rails, for example, discovers the columns and relationships in a database schema, and uses that data to build a model, view, and controller for a web application. The characteristics of the environment are striking:

- It's incredibly productive. It's easily five times as productive as the closest Java competitor, for certain types of problems.

- It is flexible. Some solutions build a default application and allow common extension points. Rails builds a default application, which you can extend as if you'd written it yourself.

- It reduces duplication, and leads to more consistency.

To me, for enterprise application development, the overriding characteristic of a language or environment is productivity. I want each line of code to work harder, and I want that to translate into productivity. I don't quit measuring productivity after deployment. If your tiny application is impossible to maintain, you'll lose everything you've gained. For these reasons, I love Ruby on Rails, and I'll talk more about it in Chapter 7.

Continuation Servers

Java web developers spend an incredible amount of time managing state, threads, and the Back button. These problems get significantly more difficult as sites get more dynamic and complex. There's been a recent resurgence in Smalltalk, and most of it centers around a framework called Seaside. Since continuations maintain state, continuation-based servers don't have any problem managing state. They also handle Back buttons and threading with relative ease. This framework uses a language feature called *continuations* to maintain state within a web-based application.

The Premise

I don't mean to say that Smalltalk or Ruby will take over the world tomorrow. I don't even mean to say that anything will ever achieve the success that Java has, again. But I don't believe that Java is permanent. For five years, it's been a good strategy to ignore the borders beyond Java, but no language will keep its leadership position forever. By now, the premise of this book should be taking shape for you:

- Java is moving away from its base. Hard-core enterprise problems may be easier to solve, but the simplest problems are getting harder to solve. And...

- Java is showing signs of wear, and interesting innovations are beginning to appear outside of Java. So...

- It's time to start paying attention again.

Pick up your eyes. Start by picking up this book. You'll be glad you did.

CHAPTER 2

The Perfect Storm

The power and the fury of the storm caught us off guard. El Niño, a weather pattern famous for producing a continuous stream of storms in Texas, seemed to misfire over and over. The core of the Austin kayaking community, dependent on storms to fuel our unfortunate addiction, sat frustrated around an ancient TV with a snowy signal, watching storm after storm split up and float completely around us. Around 11:00, everything changed. Like every day leading up to this day, a line of storms lay spread out before us like kids at a Harry Potter movie on opening day. Only this time, they punched Austin, hard.

El Niño, the split jet stream, filtered across the ocean and brought warm, moist air right across Texas. It collided with the cooler air of a cold front. The pressure system in the South fed a rotation, and locked the cool front in place. The warm air exploded into the cold and produced a perfect storm. We opened the topological maps and found a stream that had never been run. It had the steepness and geographical features that we were looking for. It simply had not had enough water. As we planned the trip, the mighty storm hurled a string of consecutive lightning bolts right near a hilltop, less than a mile away. Distracted, we stared into the night, alternately black and blinding.

Storm Warnings

To know where Java is going, you've got to know where it came from. You need to remember the conditions that caused us to leave the existing dominant languages in droves. You must understand the economic forces that drove the revolution. And you cannot forget the sentiment of the time that pried so many of us away from C++, and other programming languages for the Internet.

In 1995, Java was working its way through the labs of Sun Microsystems, unborn. Sun garnered attention as a champion of standards, and for bringing Unix out of the academic ghetto, but it was not a major player in development environments or programming languages. Frustrations, driven by economics but stemming from inadequacies in programming languages and programming models, rippled through the community in another kind of gathering storm.

Economics of Client-Server Computing

Frustration with long development cycles and inadequate user interfaces drove many companies to move off of mainframe computers. At first, the movement amounted to nothing more than a trickle. As the cost-cutting financial offices measured the software and hardware costs of IBM versus Microsoft on Intel, the trickle became a flood.

But the wave of migrating customers did not consider all the costs. The rapid movements from mainframes to Intel servers drove the first tsunami of chaos because the client-server movement hid significant costs:

- Management costs skyrocketed. It was too difficult to deploy tiny changes to hundreds of fat clients. Technologists could not figure out how to maintain the many desktop applications and frameworks necessary to make the architecture go.

- Many customers became increasingly wary of a gathering Microsoft monopoly.

- The tools of the day made it easy to get started, but did not handle complexity well. Typical customers simply could not make them scale.

Decision makers were caught between the pragmatic approach of a centrally managed solution and the adaptability and lower costs of Intel-based servers. They waited for a better solution, and the clouds darkened.

Microsoft

While developers struggled with C++, Microsoft planned to hammer the final nails in the coffin of OS/2, a competing operating system that it once created, but abandoned to IBM. So Microsoft grew in stature and influence, and it learned to cater to developers very well. Companies like IBM dominated the infrastructure groups (called IT for information technology). Microsoft didn't care. It went straight to the lines of business that used IT applications. Offering quick turnaround time with Excel macros and Visual Basic applications, it stole a large part of development mindshare across the world. Screw IT. The line of business could build the applications itself, and involve IT only after the fact, to clean up the resulting mess.

Microsoft grew, and some of the same people that lauded the end of OS/2 began to grow wary. Microsoft's dominance was a double-edged sword. You didn't have the problem of navigating through a bewildering sea of products and solutions. You didn't have the oppressive integration problems of making multiple vendors work together. You just pitched all the competition and looked to Redmond for the answers. But you had to be willing to give up other choices, and you had to live with the answers that you got. An evolving API stack moved quickly through OLE to COM to COM+. Operating systems' APIs changed from Win to Win32. New flavors and options emerged with new operating systems.

Microsoft captured a core of diligent developers more or less completely. Others bought some of the message, but cast a wary eye northwest. A growing core of developers looked openly for alternatives, like Novell's Netware or various Unix-based alternatives. Individual products, like Netscape Navigator, emerged to compete with Microsoft. The gathering storm seemed imminent.

The Internet

Thunder began to rumble in the distance, in the form of a rapidly growing Internet. In 1995, most people used the Internet to share static documents. Most dynamic sites were powered by command-line scripts through an interface called *Common Gateway Interface (CGI)*, in languages like Perl. That approach didn't seem to scale very well. While Perl was a very efficient language, applications were hard to read and difficult to maintain. And CGI started a new shell for each request, which proved prohibitively expensive. For enterprise computing, the Internet had the reputation of a limited toy, outside of scientific and academic communities.

In the mainstream, Microsoft seemed to miss the significance of the Internet, but many of the brightest minds in other places looked for ways to combine forces, to defang the dominant menace in the northwest. Market leaders always strive to protect their base through proprietary products and frameworks. Everyone else loves standards. IBM, which once built an empire on proprietary models encompassing hardware, software, and services, suddenly did an about-face, embracing every standard that it could find. It Internet-enabled its main products like its DB2 database through a product like net.data and its mainframe-based transaction engine through web-enabled emulators. Other companies also built better servers, and more efficient ways to share dynamic content. Netscape rose to prominence with a popular web browser. It looked for a way to share applications with documents, and found the answer in a fledgling language, recently renamed from Oak to Java. It started to rain.

Object Orientation

Object-oriented systems support three ideas that you now take for granted: encapsulation, inheritance, and polymorphism. For many years, the industry had been working toward object-oriented programming (OOP). They tried several times, but it never quite came together. The first major attempt was with Smalltalk. It was a highly productive environment, but when less-experienced developers tried to push it beyond its natural borders, they had problems. Initially, the early hype around OOP was counterproductive. It positioned OO languages as tools to achieve reuse, and suggested that inexperienced OOP teams could be many times more productive than their procedural counterparts.

Object-oriented software has the potential to be much less complex than procedural programming, but it takes some time to build the expertise to recognize patterns and to layer OO software in a way that makes sense. It also took the industry time to deliver educated developers. Though it now looks like OOP exploded overnight, that's not the case at all. After some early failures with languages like Smalltalk, systems programmers went back to the drawing board to deliver a less-ambitious version of an OOP language, and worked on delivering OOP concepts in a more limited way, as you see in Figure 2-1:

1. Smalltalk, invented in 1971, was successful as a research project, but did not experience the same success commercially.

2. In the late 1970s and into the 1980s, APIs for things like presentation systems began to organize the interfaces into logical actions, called *events*, around objects, like windows and controls.

3. In 1980, the United States Department of Defense commissioned the Ada programming language, which offered some of the features of OOP, like encapsulation and inheritance.

4. Companies like IBM and Microsoft delivered toolkits to let their users express object-oriented ideas in procedural languages. The most notable were IBM's System Object Model and Microsoft's Component Object Model.

5. C++ let C developers use C procedurally, and also develop object-oriented applications, side by side.

6. Java was invented, combining many of the inventions along the way.

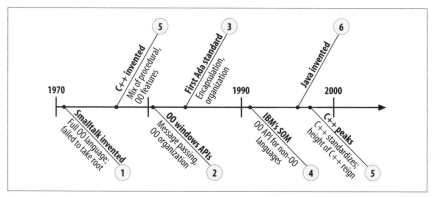

Figure 2-1. This timeline shows the slow commercial acceptance of object-oriented programming

Unfortunately, C++ came with its own sorts of problems.

The C++ Experience

As programmers wrestled with OOP, they also dealt with issues related to their chosen language. Visual Basic developers began to understand that the language and environment may be simple, but it is prone to poor performance and poor designs, leaving customers stranded with slow applications that they could not extend or maintain.

In C++, server-side developers found performance, but discovered another challenge. They did application development using a systems programming language. New terminology like *memory-stompers* and *DLL Hell* gave testament to the frustration of the masses. Simple problems dogged them.

Pointer Arithmetic

With C++, a pointer could point to any block of memory, regardless of whether it was the intention of the programmer. For example, consider the simple program in Example 2-1. It moves a block of memory from one location to another, and inverts it. Unfortunately, the example is off by 1. The code touches memory one byte beyond the `from` block. You would probably not see the error right away. You'd see it later, when you tried to manage the memory of this block, or another one. C and C++ compilers often manage memory with a linked list, and the pointers to the next block in the list sit just outside the allocated blocks! These types of errors hurt systems developers, and absolutely murdered applications developers, who didn't have the background to effectively troubleshoot these types of problems. Reliability also suffered.

Example 2-1. Move and invert a block of memory

```
// move and invert from_block into to_block with size size

int i;
for(i=0; i<size; i++) {
  to_block[size-i] = from_block[i];  // off by one!
}
```

Nested Includes

One of my most vivid and frustrating memories from working with IBM came from porting a C++ application that had include files nested 37 layers deep. It can be a very difficult problem to manage, especially for inexperienced developers.

The problem goes something like this. In C++, you specify interfaces to your methods, with other supporting information, in a header file, or *.h* file. For example, in MySQL, you have a main include file that has these includes (I've omitted most of the code for brevity):

```
#ifndef _global_h            /* If not standard header */
#include <sys/types.h>
…
#include <custom_conf.h>
…
#ifdef __LCC__
#include <winsock.h>         /* For windows */
#endif
…
#include "mysql_com.h"
#include "mysql_version.h"
```

That doesn't look so bad, until you consider that some of these includes are compiled conditionally, so you really must know which compiler directives are set before you can decide definitively whether something gets included. Also, one of your include files might include another include file, like this line in *mysql_version.h:*

```
#include <custom_conf.h>
```

In truth, this MySQL tree goes only three levels deep. It's an excellent example of how to code enterprise software in C++. It's not usually this easy. Any dependency will have an include file, and if that code also has dependencies, you'll have to make sure those include files and their associated libraries get installed and put in the right place. Lather, rinse, repeat.

Java does not have this problem at all. You deal with only one type of source file, with one kind of import, and no conditional compilation.

Strings

Many of the largest corporations used C++ for enterprise application development, even though it had very limited support for managing strings. C programs simply used arrays of characters for strings, like this:

```
char str [] = "Hello";
```

This is going to allocate a fixed-length string to str. It's merely an array of characters. And it can never hold a string longer than six characters. You could decide to use the C++ string library instead.

C++ did support the C-style string library for some string-like features. For example, to assign one string to another when the memory has already been allocated, you need to copy the bytes instead, like this:

```
strcpy (string1, string2);
```

C-style strings were ugly, dangerous, and tedious. As with any other type of pointer manipulation, you can walk off the end of a block and create an error that may not be discovered for hours or months. C++ strings are far more tedious than alternatives in languages, including Java.

Beginning in 1997, the ANSI standard for C++ introduced a more formal string. You could have a more natural representation that looked like this:

```
String str = "Hello, I'm feeling a little better.";
```

And many C++ libraries had proprietary string libraries. But the damage was done. Many programmers already knew C, and never used the C++-style strings.

DLL Hell

On Microsoft operating systems and OS/2, you compiled libraries that might depend on other libraries. The operating system linked these together with a feature called Dynamic Linking Libraries (DLLs). But the OS did not do any kind of dependency checking. As many applications share versions of the same programming libraries, it was possible, and even probable, that installing your application might replace a library that another application needed with an incompatible version. Microsoft operating systems still suffer from DLL Hell today.

CORBA

As the C++ community grew, they looked to distribute their code in ways beyond client-server. Common Object Request Broker Architecture, or CORBA, emerged quickly. With CORBA, you could build applications from objects with well-defined interfaces. You could take an object, and without adding any remoting logic you could use it on the Internet. Companies like IBM tried to push a CORBA model into every object, and companies like Iona focused only on distributed interfaces around remote objects. The kindling around CORBA began to smolder, but never really caught fire. The distribution that was so transparent and helpful was actually too easy. People built applications that relied on fine-grained communication across the wire. Too many round-trip communications led to poor performance and reputation problems for CORBA.

Inheritance Problems

C++ nudged the industry in tiny steps toward OOP, but the steps often proved awkward and counterproductive. C++ had at least three major problems:

- C++ actually did not force object orientation. You could have functions that did not belong in classes. As a result, much of the code written in C++ was not really object-oriented at all. The result was that the object-oriented C was often more like (C++)--.

- C++ did not force one root object. That led to object trees with many different roots, which proved awkward for object-oriented developers.

- C++ supported multiple inheritance. Programmers had not accumulated the wisdom born from experience to use multiple inheritance correctly. For this reason, many languages have a cleaner implementation of multiple inheritance, called a *mixin*.

Multiple inheritance is a powerful tool in the right hands, but it can lead to significant problems for the novice. Example 2-2 shows an example of multiple inheritance in action. A Werewolf is part Man and part Wolf. Problems arise when both Man and Wolf inherit from a common class, called Mammal. If Werewolf then inherits a method introduced in Mammal, it's ambiguous whether Werewolf would inherit through Man or Wolf, as in Figure 2-2. This problem, known as the *diamond inheritance problem*, illustrates just one of the problems related to multiple inheritance.

Example 2-2. Multiple inheritance in C++

```
class Werewolf: public Man, public Wolf
```

Multiple inheritance is like any power tool. It gives you leverage and speed and can save you time, but you've got to have enough knowledge and experience to use it safely and effectively to keep all your fingers and toes. Most developers using C++ as an applications language had neither.

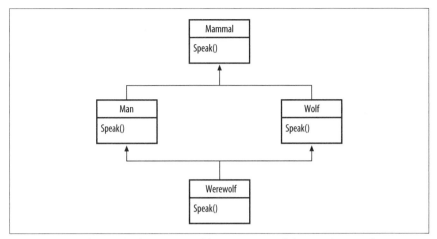

Figure 2-2. The diamond inheritance problem is just one of the complexities that can arise with multiple inheritance

Consistency

Like Perl, C++ is most definitely an expressive language, but that flexibility comes at an incredible cost. C++ is full of features that might make sense to a seasoned developer, but that have catastrophic effects at runtime. For example, = often doubles as an assignment and a test. Most new developers will get burned by this problem. It takes years and years of study and experience to become proficient with C++. For systems development, that makes sense, because you ultimately need the performance and control inherent in the ability to put every byte where you want to. Applications developers simply don't want to deal with those low-level details.

Portability

Most developers expected C++ to be more portable, but it didn't turn out that way. We were buried under mountains of incompatible libraries, and inconsistencies between libraries on different platforms. C++ left so much in the hands of the vendors implementing the spec that C++ turned out to be one of the least portable languages ever developed. In later years, problems got so bad that you often couldn't link a library built by different versions of the same compiler, let alone different operating systems.

Like mud accumulating on a boot, the language that once looked so cool on a resume began to weigh down the brightest developers, and stymie lesser developers completely. Instead of moving to a limited language like Visual Basic or Power Builder, they waited, and the storm clouds grew darker still.

Compromises

You don't get a perfect storm without all the conditions. The primary success in the initial Java explosion was based on the extraordinary migration of the C++ community. To do this, Java had to walk a tightrope with excellent balance. C++ had some obvious warts, like an awkward syntax, multiple inheritance, primitives rather than objects, typing models, poor strings, and awkward libraries. In some cases, Sun decided to opt for a simpler, cleaner applications language. Java's research roots as an embedded language drove a simplicity that served it well. In other cases, it opted to cater conservatively to the C++ community.

It's easy to look at Java now and criticize the founders for decisions made, but it's clear to me that they walked the tightrope very well. The rapid growth of the hype around Java and the community allowed a success that none of us could have possibly predicted. All of this happened amid an all-out war between Microsoft and IBM! If Java had stopped at this point, it would have been successful. But it didn't stop here. Not by a long shot.

Clouds Open

The sound and fury of the Java storm caught many of us off-guard. And why not? It came from an unlikely source, was delivered in an unconventional vehicle, and defied conventional wisdom regarding performance of interpreted languages. Other than the language, nothing about Java was conventional at all, including the size of the explosion. In retrospect, you can look back and see just how well it filled a void. Figure 2-3 shows the many ingredients that come together to form the perfect storm.

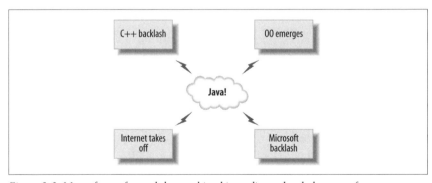

Figure 2-3. Many forces formed the combined ingredients that led to a perfect storm

New Economics

The jet stream that powered this storm emerged from a series of standards: TCP/IP, HTTP, URI, and HTML. The Internet gathered steam, and Sun took full advantage with Java. The Internet was everywhere. Java was cool. The Java developers quickly built the API set that would allow developers to code for the Internet, including TCP/IP APIs for communication, and applets for building user interfaces that you could embed in a browser. JDBC allowed database access.

The perfect combination formed by the relationship between Netscape Navigator and Java drove each company to new heights. Through Netscape, Sun was able to put Java in front of an incredible number of developers, nearly instantaneously. Through Java, Netscape could showcase smart applications that looked cool, and were simultaneously practical. The Navigator/Java combination seemingly solved the most critical problems of client-server computing: management and distribution. If you could install a browser, you could then automatically distribute any application that you wanted through the browser. Java had the perfect economic conditions for success. Java found an important ally in the bean counters that liked the manageability of the green screen, but the productivity and usability of the fat client.

Customers wanted solutions, and Sun realized that Java would give them what they wanted. Sun immediately saw the opportunity it faced. With the open standards around the Internet and the Java language powering it, Solaris on Sun servers would be a compelling, and even hip, alternative. Above all, Java made Sun safe. Because its virtual machine ran in a browser and on many different operating systems, some hard decisions didn't seem so hard. You could try out a deployment scenario. If you didn't like it, you could just move on.

The new jet stream was in position to feed power to the growing storm.

C++ on Prozac

When Lucene founder Doug Cutting called Java *C++ on Prozac*,[*] I immediately liked the comparison. Because of its C++ syntax, Java found an impressive waiting community of developers looking for a solution. They moved to add a hip Java, and Internet experience, to their resumes. They stayed because they liked it. Java had most of the benefits of C++, without

---

[*] TheServerSide.com, "Doug Cutting—Founder of Lucene and Nutch," Tech Talk (March 10, 2005); *http://www.theserverside.com/talks/videos/DougCutting/interview.tss*.

the problems. The similarities of the languages made it easy to learn. And Java was liberating, for many reasons:

- Java provided more structure in places that needed it, such as providing interfaces instead of inheritance.
- Java eliminated the burden of pointers, improving stability and readability.
- Garbage collection got easier, because the JVM automatically took care of abandoned references.
- Java allowed a much better packaging mechanism, and simplified the use of libraries.
- Java cleaned up problems like nested include files and macros.

Architecture

The benefits of Java went beyond economics and C++. I can still vaguely remember the first sentence that I saw describing Java. Sun said it was a portable, safe, secure, object-oriented, distributed programming language for the Internet. Those words were all buzzwords of the time. For C++ developers, Java underpinnings made significant strides:

- The JVM allowed unprecedented portability. Many experts believe that the JVM, and not the language, is the most important feature of Java. Sun marketed this capability brilliantly with the acronym *WORA*. Java developers the world over recognize those letters as standing for Write Once, Run Anywhere.
- Java published the byte code specification for the JVM. People who want to build their own JVM or build a language on the existing JVM standard can do so, or even modify byte codes of existing applications. Frameworks like JDO do modify byte code with great success.
- While C++ allowed unrestricted access to application memory, Java restricted access to one area of the JVM called the *sandbox*. Even today, you see very few exploitations of Java security.
- The Java metamodel, made up of the class objects that describe types in Java, allowed sophisticated reflective programming. Though it's a little awkward, the capabilities of Java extend far beyond the basic capabilities of C++. The Java metamodel enables frameworks that increase transparency, like Hibernate (persistence) and Spring (services such as remoting and transactions).

- The fathers of Java saw the importance of security, and baked it into the language. Java introduced a generation of programmers to the term *sandbox*, which limited the scope and destructive power of applications.
- Java had improved packaging and extensibility. You could effectively drop in extensions to Java that transparently added to capabilities of a language. You could use different types of archives to package and distribute code.

Both the low-level grunts and high-level architects had something to love. Businesspeople had a motivation to move. At this point, if all else had failed, Java would have been a successful language. But it didn't fail. The winds just kept picking up speed, and the storm started feeding on itself.

Fury Unleashed

Applets captured the imagination of programmers everywhere. They solved the deployment problem, they were cool, and they were easy to build. We're only now finding a set of technologies, based on the ugly and often objectionable JavaScript language, that can build rich content for the Web as well as Java did. Still, applets started to wane.

Even today, I think that applets represent a powerful idea, but they fizzled out for many reasons. The Netscape browser's JVM was buggy and unpredictable. Further, with such a rapidly evolving language, applets presented many of the same problems that client-server computing did. You may not have to maintain applications, but you still had to maintain the browser. After you'd deployed a few Java applets, you had to worry about keeping the right version of the browser on the desktop. As the size of the JVM grew, it became less and less likely that you could install a JVM remotely. Even if you could, Java versions came out often enough, and were different enough, that new applications frequently needed to materialize. But a few mad scientists at Sun were up to the challenge again.

James Duncan Davidson: Why Java Won

Author of *The Rise of Java*

James Duncan Davidson is a freelance computer programmer, photographer, author, and speaker. He invented both Ant and Tomcat, two of the most successful Java open source projects ever. His persistent efforts at Sun led to open sourcing both projects. He is now one of the best-selling authors of Apple operating system books.

What do you like best about Java?

JDD: At the time, it seemed like a really good idea. Mostly, for what Java was designed for, they got it right. Of course, it's a strongly typed language, which for some purposes is great, and other purposes not.

Why do you think it's so successful?

JDD: I think it comes down to the fact that server-side programming in Perl and the like was inefficient, and server-side programming in C and C++ was hard. Java, and servlets in particular, busted open a door for Java where it could really take root.

I may be biased because of my involvement with servlets, but Java without the server side wasn't that interesting. It still isn't. Sure, J2ME is on bazillions of mobile devices, but there aren't that many apps there—and the APIs there are limited unless you actually make the cell phone.

What don't you like?

JDD: Strong typing. Reliance on APIs rather than frameworks. That's a subtle but important distinction. The increasing complexity of even basic APIs. For example, you can't just write a servlet anymore, you have to write a servlet, then edit an XML file. They're killing off the approachability that helped servlets get off the ground. With it, the rest of the server stack gets more and more difficult to work with.

And reliance on tools to make it easy is a cop-out.

As well, I don't like the massive monolithic approach to "Editions." Most people don't need J2EE. They need a web container. End of story.

I also don't like the incredible jump to complexity that Java seems to engender in people. No other platform has grown as fast and as elephantine as Java. Other platforms are as capable, but are 5% of the size. There's an architectural reason for that. And, really, Java the language isn't at fault. Java the class libraries are. They encourage massively inefficient design. Ever see a stack trace come out of a JSP/servlet/J2EE container? The 44 pages of stack call should be a hint.

How does Java hold you back? **JDD:** It doesn't. I don't use Java much anymore. I use other languages like Python, Ruby, and ObjC.

And I wish that more tools would just remember the lessons of Unix: small pieces loosely joined. There is no one übersolution, and at the end of the day, if you can take two tools and pipe stuff between them, you have a more powerful and flexible solution than any monolithic beast. And one in which users can discover uses far more powerful than you can imagine.

What emerging alternatives make sense to you, if any? **JDD:** Ruby on Rails has picked up an amazing amount of traction for server-side stuff. If you need to slush around mass amounts of content, there are content databases (like MarkLogic) that are interesting that use XQuery to work with the stuff inside. On the GUI front, well, Java wasn't a contender, so everything is already an alternative.

What would prompt (or did prompt) you to move away from Java, or .NET? **JDD:** I shifted focus into the GUI application space. Java and GUIs don't mix. Friends don't let friends Swing.

Servlets

As applets were winding down on the client side, the server side was just getting going. Servlets gave Java developers a way to write applications that would run in the browser. An application would get a request over HTTP, and build a plain web page, with no Java, that would return to the client. Since the web pages were built server side, they could take dynamic content, like the results of database queries, back down to the client. So-called web-based applications finally delivered the goods: now, you could run enterprise applications on a client. You'd only have to deploy them on a server.

It didn't take long to understand that the clients could be within the firewalls of a company, but they didn't have to be. Since people everywhere had

Internet access, it opened up the possibility of selling a whole new kind of product: information. The new economy was born. At least in part, it was powered by Java, and the companies that built the servers, databases, and software. Start-up companies sprung up to take advantage of this opportunity. Enormous paper wealth was created. Venture capitalists funded good ideas and bad. A drive for customers fed the fury of the storm. The rules were simple: he who gets the most customers wins. Start-ups were often willing to spend far more to acquire a customer than that customer could possibly generate.

Real wealth was created, too. Companies like eBay and Amazon fueled a new kind of economy without buildings or walls. This new sophisticated commerce drove a new need for new tools. Sun, Oracle, BEA, and IBM worked on new standards to enable enterprise on the Web. IBM coined the term *e-business* to stand for a new, powerful way to serve customers.

J2EE

J2EE, or Java's enterprise edition, included many new ways to connect to the enterprise. Under great expectations, the Enterprise JavaBeans™ (EJB) spec emerged to add a rich set of tools that would let you program distributed, transactional, secure, and persistent applications, without coding those services yourself. Clustering features enabled good scalability and reliability. These features let major companies move into the Java world without reservation.

Though EJB never quite fulfilled its promise, the specification is an extraordinary example of how an idea can energize a community. The specifications behind EJB are tremendously important, and for the most part, are factored very well. Java thrived on the server side and was off to the races again.

Industry Standards

It's tough to unite through common interests. Java never could have thrived to the extent that it has with only Sun behind it. Some unifying force needed to hold them together. A common enemy in Microsoft was the perfect catalyst.

Software is more prone to monopolies than most other industries because software moves fast and obsolescence can devastate a company. For this reason, market share tends to favor the market leader heavily. So it stands to reason that market leaders love to be proprietary. They can increase market share through their leadership position, and lock their customers in to extend the monopoly. Certainly, Microsoft is not the first company to use this strategy. IBM was incredibly proficient at this game.

If being proprietary works for the market leader, the followers need open standards to level the playing field. If you can't build dominant share, you can lend your customer safety by creating partnerships and embracing a common standard. In this way, your customers are not nearly as afraid of obsolescence.

The Unix operating system helped smaller proprietary server vendors survive for years in the face of market dominance by Intel and Microsoft. After supporting proprietary systems aggressively for decades, IBM is embracing open standards in many areas, including relational databases (where it trails Oracle), operating systems (where it made mainframes a much safer solution with the open source Linux environment), and now, with Java.

IBM is now the most prevalent Java developer. It claims to have more Java developers than any other company, including Sun. I believe IBM. It has been working to catch BEA's Web Logic application server for years, and has now passed BEA. I'd expect IBM to exercise its dominance to build in proprietary features that interest its customers. I would also expect IBM to take a harder line with the Java Community Process (JCP), to force through changes that it finds most interesting. Failing that, it may leave the JCP and seek another avenue for establishing standards. If it does, this strategy should not come as a surprise. It's the prerogative of the market leader, and the dance goes on.

Open Source

Many open source communities look down on Java. That's ironic, because Java has more thriving open source software than any of the alternatives. When you build something that's both hip and popular, people want to play with it and share their creations. Add a massive community that's stretching a language in unexpected ways, and you need only to stand back and watch interesting things happen. And boy, did Java open source happen.

At first, Sun resisted the open source community. Sun developer, James Duncan Davidson, worked to change that. He built two of the most important Java applications ever in Tomcat (that showcased servlets) and Ant (that builds nearly all Java applications today). He then pushed them out to the open source community.

The typical open source development cycle works as follows (and shown in Figure 2-4):

1. **Build.** Once Java geeks solve a problem often enough, they often build the solution with their own resources. Sometimes, they're solving business problems. Other times, they're just having fun.

2. **Use.** Users then exercise the solution. Those that don't get used atrophy and die.

3. **Refine.** Users then refine the solution, to match their requirements.

4. **Contribute.** Users then contribute to the project, either with feedback or with code enhancements. They are willing to do so, because they won't have to maintain enhancements.

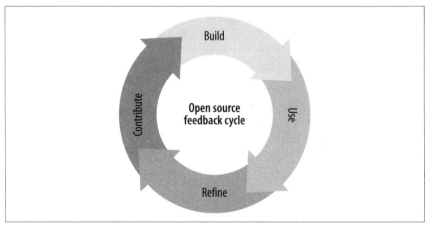

Figure 2-4. The open source feedback cycle is tremendously important to Java

In this way, some fantastic frameworks evolved to form the foundation of Java web-based development. Today, you'd be hard-pressed to find a major company that does not take advantage of open source software. These solutions are pervasive in the Java community:

- Developers use JUnit to build automated test cases, which run with every build.

- IT shops run Apache Web Server as their preferred web server.

- Customers deploy many lightweight applications with Tomcat as a servlet container.

- Developers look to Hibernate for persistence.

- Web-based developers use Struts to separate model, view, and controller layers of their applications.

- Programmers worldwide use Ant to build applications.

- Other frameworks like Lucene (search), Spring (infrastructure), Tapestry (web-based component design), JBoss (J2EE), and many others seem to be gaining popularity as well.

You might think that open source development would threaten software companies that build software, but the converse is true. Open source has served Java very well. Innovation in the open source community keeps tremendous pressure on software companies to keep up. That's healthy. If you're providing real value, you'll thrive. If you try to live off of technology that's well understood and popular, you'll die. Open source software raises the bar of what you've got to do to make money. IBM has dealt with the pressure well. BEA is withering under the heat, with IBM above and JBoss below. Either you will see BEA innovate, or an open source framework like JBoss, Geronimo, or Spring will catch it on the low end. Either way, you'll win.

You could even argue that open source software is driving the most important innovation in the Java space. Open source is driving adoption and implementation of integrated development environments, aspect-oriented programming, lightweight containers, persistence, unit testing, and the best web MVC frameworks. It's driving the actions of the largest and most powerful Java vendors. That's an incredible testament to the might of the Java open source community.

Aftermath

I believe that Java is now the most successful programming language ever. It redefined the way we package and deliver software. It changed the way we feel about interpreted languages, and the way we build Internet applications. Java changed the very economics of application development by bringing deployment and management into the overall equation. It built a new affinity for libraries, with strong web-based support. Java ushered in a massive wave of important standards that now form the very foundation of enterprise software development. Java has changed the rules of the game— Java completely rewrote the rulebook defining what it takes to be a commercially successful programming language.

In some ways, Java's new rulebook will serve us well. To achieve similar success, a new language will need to be portable and encourage a vibrant open source community. It will need broad appeal, across low-level programmers and architects. It will need to embrace compelling standards.

But technology is only part of the problem. For a new language to succeed, you'll also need a compelling business reason to switch. In some ways, Java held us back by discouraging competition. You may be tempted to use Java, even if it's the wrong tool for the job. You may work harder than you have to, because you're not free to explore alternatives. And this situation may lure us into a false sense of security, just as so many Java developers feel so comfortable wholly inside Java's cocoon.

Moving Ahead

We may never again see a perfect storm like the one that ushered in Java. You shouldn't look for one. Instead, you should learn from the success of Java, and start to understand the factors that led to its success. Minimally, I believe the next commercially successful programming language will need to satisfy four major criteria:

- It will need to establish a significant community. You won't see broad adoption unless the adopter can achieve relative safety.
- It will need to be portable. Java's virtual machine has raised the bar for languages that follow.
- Some economic incentive must justify the movement. Currently, productivity to me looks like the logical economic force, but others may be lurking out there, like wireless computing or data search.
- It will need demonstrable technical advantages. This is actually the least important of the major criteria.

I don't think most of us can possibly thoroughly understand the success of Java. It's easy to overestimate the role of the language and to underestimate the importance of the JVM and the community. In the next chapter, we'll continue to look at the crown jewels of Java in more detail, or the foundation for the most successful programming language ever.

CHAPTER 3

Crown Jewels

After the sixth drop in 40 minutes, I looked back up the river, and reflected. I was colder than I'd ever been. I hadn't eaten in six hours. My head and back hurt, and I was afraid—in short, pure bliss. Despite the painfully long hikes with a boat cutting into my shoulder, and the fear of facing a wall of water barely covering rocks that have maimed or even killed before, and the ubiquitous smell of wet neoprene every evening, I can't get enough. Kayaking delivers me to places that nothing else can reach. The immediate feedback tells me exactly how I'm doing. Others can't do it for me, but others can tell me how to do it for myself. And the feeling of conquering a tiny piece of river is incredible.

Java was once like that for me. I get enormous productivity jolts out of Java's incredible community, and countless open source projects. The open standards and the JVM mean that my knowledge, and my applications, can move from place to place. Java's been tremendously successful. You've seen my views about why it was popular. If you're to understand what might possibly come after Java, you need to ask questions about Java's continued success:

- What makes Java hip, and draw such a wide variety of people?
- How has the open source community thrived, in times, despite Sun and the power vendors?
- What are the indispensable technical underpinnings that make Java successful?
- What makes Java so adaptable that programmers can build everything from web sites to databases?

Answers to these questions go well beyond one single brain. To provide a better answer, I interviewed dozens of the top Java developers and asked them what made Java so successful. Table 3-1 shows some of the interesting answers.

Table 3-1. Reasons for Java's success according to top Java consultants

Consultant	Why was Java so successful?
James Duncan Davidson	I think it comes down to the fact that server-side programming in Perl and the like was inefficient; server-side programming in C and C++ was hard. Java and servlets in particular busted open a door for Java where it could really take root.
Jason Hunter	It allowed you to do something that couldn't be done in any other way, and that was applets. Applets in and of themselves didn't end up as an important technology, but they provided Java with a protective beachhead where it could initially establish itself without any serious competitors.
Dennis Sosnoski	Java has a well-designed language and runtime environment. Prior to 1.5, it also had the advantage of being relatively clean and easy to teach.
Stuart Halloway	It was better than C++.
Richard Monson-Haefel	Java is a great static object-oriented programming language. It's portable and has loads of APIs, products, and open source projects. It is a well-designed language and virtual machine. Initially, it was a very progressive and well-timed language design. Also, portability was big. Today, it's simply everywhere, which is why it continues to grow in popularity.
Ramnivas Laddad	Java allowed a widespread and mainstream acceptance of garbage collection and reflection. Although these concepts existed forever, mainstream developers didn't really use them until Java. Also, Java achieved platform independence to a reasonable level.

Now, you can start to see a clearer picture. From the answers in Table 3-1, several threads emerge:

- The technical bar for success was not too high. Since so many were developing business applications in C++, which is a systems language, Java needed only to improve on that experience to succeed.
- The ability to develop enterprise applications was critical. James Duncan Davidson suggests that the central enterprise problem of the time was enabling for the Internet.
- The technical underpinnings of the language, especially the JVM, represented a significant step forward.
- The importance of community represents a significant achievement of Java.
- Applets may have been the killer app that launched Java.

If you compare these comments in 2005 to similar comments made in 1997, you see a few notable differences: Java's exception strategy and static typing may be a hindrance rather than a help; Java's productivity may no longer be as good as it once was; Java has had a bigger impact on the server than on the client; and Java is not as simple as it once was. Still, Java experts remain remarkably consistent in terms of the importance of the JVM, community, Internet development, and improvements over C++.

Language and JVM Design

In 1996, the JVM represented a significant departure from traditional thinking. Overwhelmingly, organizations exclusively used high-performance compiled languages on the server side. Developers patched on security instead of baking it in from the beginning. And vendors attempted to achieve portability by building extensive libraries at a very high level. Instead of driving on this well-traveled road, they reached for the steering wheel with both hands and threw all of their momentum to the side, swerving aggressively into unpaved, uncharted territory.

Portability

In the early and mid-1990s, many in the industry were just starting to think about portability. In particular, I vividly remember working on object-oriented technologies at IBM. The project, called System Object Model (SOM), emerged from a research project that formed the foundation for OS/2's groundbreaking object-oriented desktop, and some experimental technologies that never made it out of the lab. The goals of SOM were ambitious: we wanted to build a common object model underneath as many object-oriented languages as possible. Then, we could develop a common suite of libraries that developers could use across languages and operating systems. Over time, we discovered the difficulties of porting a technology across many operating systems and programming languages. Of course, the technical challenges were daunting, but the political challenges turned out to be insurmountable. We immediately discarded the Smalltalk-like integrated development machine and the virtual machine, concepts introduced by Smalltalk and Lisp, because a VM couldn't possibly be fast enough. We weren't alone in our approach. Many C++-driven companies tried to build programming libraries across many languages. Few succeeded.

The Java approach, shown in Figure 3-1, is fundamentally different. Java's virtual machine simply redefines the machine, providing a lower-level, firmer foundation for portability. Java designers bet that they could overcome performance concerns. It was not a new idea; nor was it a popular one. Over time, they proved to be right—just-in-time compilers improved performance so that the overhead of the JVM became acceptable, and even rivaled compiled languages. The virtual machine, built into Netscape Navigator, proved to be a fantastic launching pad for the Java platform. It's enabled Java to extend into the realm of mobile devices, application servers, and countless software products. When all is said and done, popularizing the idea of the VM may be the most important technical contribution of Java.

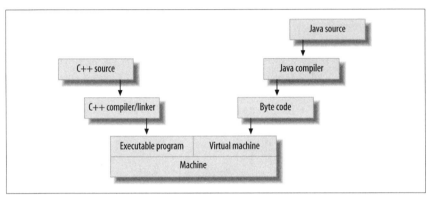

Figure 3-1. The JVM took a different approach to performance, security, and portability; most programming languages use compilers to bind them to individual machines, but Java simply redefined the machine

Java offers a rich set of interfaces that often delve into operating system territory. Under the covers, Java either implements this type of functionality from scratch, or just calls the native features underneath. Either way, Java developers can count on a rich, consistent library wherever they are. In almost 10 years of software development, though I've seen minor annoyances, I've rarely encountered major problems in porting from one operating system to another. In the end, Sun didn't invent the VM, but Sun did make the VM popular.

Java portability is not without its problems. Graphical user interfaces pose a particularly sticky problem: is it important to maintain portability even at the expense of consistency with the operating system underneath? For example, Swing components, not operating system components, implement the menus in a Java GUI. This arrangement causes problems on the Apple platforms, where the menu for an application traditionally is implemented as a single bar on top of the desktop, instead of the separate menu per application that you commonly see on Unix and Windows. Other notable differences, like security and threading, show up differently on different operating systems. Even filenames can present problems, where having two classes called *Account.txt* and *account.txt* would be legal on Unix but not on Windows. But for the most part, Java handles portability very well.

Security

In the age of the Internet, security takes on an entirely new level of importance. Any ubiquitous technology must deal with it, and deal with it well. Sun's engineers recognized this and dealt with the threat from the very beginning. They were fortunate to have the virtual machine to simplify the problem. Unfortunately, other vendors were not so lucky.

Changing threats

Microsoft Windows has been besieged with security problems. The Internet and email make a perfect medium for viruses to spread with frightening speed. Dominant market share, combined with huge holes in Windows and its browsers, make them the target of most Internet viruses.

In fact, blatant security holes in Windows have led to a whole new type of security threat, called *adware*. Five years ago, it didn't exist. Today, I found 6 million Google hits on the term! As you probably know, adware seeks to exploit vulnerabilities in Internet Explorer to drive up traffic to certain sites and learn about the activities of a user. Most analysts believe that adware has usurped the virus as the top security threat, because these often malicious applications spread so broadly and so quickly. They often lower security settings to enable other types of more serious attacks.

C and C++ also present enormous security concerns. C++ applications have full access to operating system APIs and unrestricted access to every byte in their dedicated memory space. Many versions of the Windows operating system cannot protect one application from another. Given the Internet as the ultimate delivery vehicle through components like ActiveX you can quickly develop unacceptable levels of risk. Given the sensitivity of the data that many of us keep on our machines, these threats take on a more serious dimension.

Remedies in Java

The virtual machine gave Java designers a chance to have a secure foundation on an insecure platform. The advantages deal primarily with the restricted sandbox:

- Since Sun designed Java from the ground up, it did not need to worry about patching legacy security problems, like those you might find in

Unix and Windows. (These are operating systems, but they also are application platforms.)

- Java, the language and the JVM, grew up after the Internet, so the inventors had the benefit of knowing what types of attacks might occur.
- Java has a security manager built in at the lowest level, to enforce security policy and to control access to low-level system priorities.
- The JVM provides a limited sandbox for a group of Java applications, so a malicious or buggy application can't do as much damage as, say, a C++ application might.
- Because there's no pointer arithmetic, and because Java has strong runtime typing, the JVM knows precisely where a reference is pointing. The JVM can better restrict an application's access to its own memory. Most Java security attacks try to defeat type safety first.

The relative dearth of Java security breaches represents perhaps the biggest compliment to Java's founders. It's just a tough environment for viruses, or adware, or security attacks. The base operating system makes a much riper target.

Moving Forward

The idea of the virtual machine is here to stay. The intermediate virtual machine transforms the basic problems of portability, security, and deployment from nearly unsolvable to routine. If the virtual machine adapts to accept dynamic languages, the JVM will probably be the deployment platform of choice for the foreseeable future. If not, a new virtual machine will need to emerge.

But the problem of portability has proven to be a difficult one. Jython, a dynamic language based on Python but running in the JVM, never quite reached the expected level of prominence in the Python community, particularly because it wasn't fast enough, and partly because the Python community never embraced it. A project to implement Ruby on the JVM, called JRuby, has similar difficulties so far. Still, many analysts predict that the JVM will live long beyond the time that the last Java developer writes the last, lonely line of code.

I'm convinced that the next major programming language will be much more dynamic. It's pretty clear that newer dynamic languages will also have the benefit of a virtual machine. If the lax sales of security books and Windows alternatives are any indication, security just doesn't mean as much to us as we think it does. Still, alternatives may have the benefit of Java's virtual machine. If not, cross your fingers. The next major alternative may not be as secure as Java, because most language designers don't start by building in security first. Until we fix fundamental holes in our processes, our thinking, and our operating systems, security in the languages built on top won't matter much.

The Internet

C evolved from a systems language built to create operating systems. It's a systems programming language. C, and the C++ follow-up language, didn't creep into the enterprise until later. Unlike C++, a very early target for Java was mobile computing, and it evolved very quickly to encompass Internet applications for the enterprise. You can easily see Sun's intentions in four primary places:

- Java included convenience features to make applications programming easier. Java added garbage collection and memory management, so application developers wouldn't have to deal with these issues. Java included first-class strings, so the platform, rather than the programmer, could deal with moving the individual bytes around. A systems language might want more control.

- Java's vision for enterprise computing was centered on the Internet. Java built in several libraries that greatly simplified enterprise computing and the growing language always kept the Internet as a central focus. Early APIs enabled everything from communications protocols like TCP/IP sockets to the applet framework that allowed embedded applications in a browser.

- Java's fathers keenly moved to improve simplicity, at the price of low-level flexibility. For example, though C++ could touch any byte in the system, they knew that the C++ applications community struggled with pointer arithmetic.

- Very early, Java was targeted at mobile applications, but Sun saw an opportunity to topple Microsoft. Sun took the opportunity, extending the primary focus of Java into the Internet.

Remember this: client/server computing made it very difficult to deploy applications. Thousands of Windows clients, and a distributed network of hundreds of servers to power them, were cheaper than mainframes to buy, but they were horrendously expensive to manage. In the late 1990s, corporate visions changed from client/server computing to networks of applications built with Internet standards, called intranets, existing entirely inside corporate boundaries. When Sun embedded Java into the first version of Netscape Navigator, this vision looked quite possible.

A Consistent Evolving Vision

The ultimate goal for the Internet is this: give all users a single application platform (we call it a browser), and give them the ability to run applications in it. Initially, those applications took the form of applets. It was a simple idea—embed the JVM into a browser, and let the user just download Java byte code that makes up an applet as one more message (MIME) type. The browser would just hand the applet to the JVM. Initially, many companies deployed their first few applets with great success. Later, applets fell out of favor. Over the course of my interviews for this book, I found broadly different views of why they failed:

- Deployment was hard. Applet developers discovered that they had traded one problem—deploying operating system upgrades and client applications—for another—deploying the ever-changing browsers, and synchronizing virtual machines.

- Programming was hard. Applet developers had a hard time understanding an alien programming model, and integrating the applets seamlessly with the web page. Applets done well were often magnificent, but not many applets were done well.

- The Netscape JVM was buggy. Some said that the buggy Netscape JVM killed applets single-handedly. If Netscape had better supported the notion of a pluggable virtual machine, applets might have had a better chance at success.

For whatever reason, applets faded into the background. But Java is a surprisingly nimble beast, at times. In the halls of Netscape, server-side Java emerged. *Servlets* (a term originally coined by O'Reilly) made server-driven Internet applications available to application developers. Sun capitalized on this movement quickly with a standard, and an open source implementation of a servlet engine called Tomcat. Servlets solved many of the problems of CGI-based applications, and enterprise developers had a new way to deliver applications to a desktop. The vision of an application in a browser remained, but the view logic had moved from client to server.

The server would build dynamic content and serve it to the client. Ironically, this "new" model was little more than a glorified green screen that you might find on a mainframe terminal or emulator. It did have some important subtle advantages:

- While green screens were stodgy and old, the Internet was cool and new. Users knew how to use them because they had the Internet at home. They liked to use the new systems as much as developers liked to build them.

- Browsers lacked the raw productivity of keyboard-driven interfaces, but it was much easier to train users on them. The user interfaces provided several subtle enhancements, like navigating through links instead of typing menu choices.

- The server-side development environments were much more productive than their mainframe counterparts. Development environments, often Windows clients, were much cheaper.

Java's client-side development stagnated. Swing has long been criticized for providing a poor user experience, but the real limitations lie in the learning curves and ultimately the productivity of developers that must grab it by the throat and shake to merely coax a minimal application out of it.

But Java's emphasis quickly moved wholly to the server side, where it remains today. Java Server Pages (JSP) continued the evolution, making it easier for traditional designers to play a role in the development of web applications. More modular designs, with JSP tag libraries, portal components (called *portlets*), and MVC frameworks, continued the evolution. None of Java's user interface technologies has succeeded on the same scale of web-based applications, driven from servlets.

Moving Forward

The vision of Internet applications is not yet complete. Google is now experimenting with Ajax, which seeks to provide a better experience to users with generated JavaScript and XML that communicates with the server. Applications like Google Maps show that it's possible to create richer applications with JavaScript and active communication between the client and server, but we desperately need a new user interface technology providing the advantages of easily deployed servlets and the richness of applets. JavaScript is broadly available, but it's a haphazard, problem-prone scripting language that's different on each different browser.

My intuition tells me that the ultimate answer won't look much like a browser, but will have many of the same characteristics. You can well imagine that a better marriage between a browser and a dynamic language would make it much easier to give the user a richer experience. One thing to me is clear. The Java community has not had much success with richer clients. The mainstream rich client technologies of Swing and the Standard Widget

Toolkit (SWT) keep the programmer at a very low level. Microsoft and Apple both have much better frameworks. While Java does do web-based development very well, increasingly users will demand a richer experience as they have access to more bandwidth and ultimately see the incredible power that a richer experience can unleash.

Enterprise Integration

As the emphasis in Java shifted from the client to the server (Figure 3-2), enterprise integration became more important. Here, the partnership of IBM, Oracle, BEA, Borland, Sun, and others paid huge dividends. They enabled Java connectivity to databases, transaction engines, messaging systems, and any other enterprise system that required a Java connection. The combination of vendor cooperation and support drove cooperation in standards and proliferation of useful connectors that we've never seen before. Java proved to be a good integration platform. Because of the backing of all the heavyweights, Java also became a very safe solution.

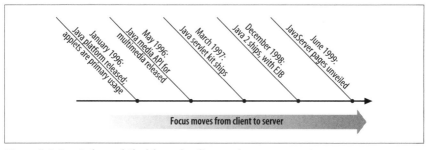

Figure 3-2. Java's focus shifted from the client to the server over time[a]

[a] Dates taken from "The Java Platform, Five Years in Review"; http://java.sun.com/features/2000/06/time-line.html. © 1994–2005 Sun Microsystems, Inc.

Java remains a good language for enterprise integration projects, because of the high number of frameworks that solve so many of the critical problems, like distributed transaction processing. Static typing is much more important for problems on a massive scale, since such problems are harder to test, bugs become more expensive. Relative to C++, in this space, the speed of authoring is more important than the speed of execution, because most execution time is spent inside of the various enterprise transaction, database, and networking libraries.

Moving Forward

Today, Java can talk to just about any enterprise system that's important to you. Beyond integration, Java now provides excellent facilities for mapping object-oriented models to relational databases. You can do distributed coordination of transactions, and manage massive messaging systems with first-class rules engines and workflow. You can reach beyond Java into C++ using a native wrapper called the Java Native Interface (JNI), or using coarse-grained strategies like web services. You've got dozens of remoting strategies available, from the 1990s standard CORBA to the Java-only RMI. Or, you might decide to use many of the lightweight HTTP strategies for remoting and web services. Different standards and free frameworks will help you manage the services for your business objects, do text-based searches, write games, or even write mobile applications.

This is the massive front that a challenger must conquer. But Java has a critical weakness, too. The easy Enterprise problems have been solved, so the key vendors spend most of their time working on the hard problems. That presents a problem for the at-large programmer. As Java moves into increasingly complex places, it has a tendency to leave the programmers of the more basic problems behind. EJBs, the intense proliferation of XML, and the massive web services stacks are just three examples of ever-increasing complexity.

In the end, Java is sacrificing its primary base, exchanging what was productive and hip for something that is tedious and slow, but powerful. Many applications don't need any of the extra enterprise stuff. I'd guess that as many as half of all commercial applications involve a web frontend that baby-sits a plain old relational database. A challenger in that space need not try to make a frontal assault. It need only provide a much more productive solution to a niche problem than Java. Watch a framework called Ruby on Rails. Its sweet spot is the web-based UI on a database. Still today, that's a tremendously important problem. It lets you capture and share information, which can in turn be used in any way imaginable.

Erik Hatcher: Java's Success
Coauthor of *Java Development with Ant*

Erik coauthored Java Development with Ant and Lucene in Action (http://lucenebook.com/). He commits on several open source projects, primarily at the Apache Software Foundation where he also serves as a member. Erik once kayaked with Bruce, barely living to tell the tale.

What do you like best about Java?

EH: It has lots of built-in capabilities and a cornucopia of third-party (meaning open source for me) libraries.

What don't you like?

EH: I sympathize with newcomers to the Java "platform." We all know Java the language is pretty easy to grasp, and that makes it seem like it won't be too hard, but in reality, you cannot build even the most trivial utility in Java without a pretty hefty learning curve.

CLASSPATH gets us all, for example; even the "experts." To really do something useful you have to learn tons more—Ant, servlet containers, JMS, JDBC, and a zillion other things. It scares me just to think of this massive beast I've somehow spent the last five years of my life on.

How does Java hold you back?

EH: I don't feel held back with it personally, but I often feel that it takes more time than it should to accomplish a particular task.

What would prompt (or did prompt) you to move away from Java, or .NET?

EH: If Ruby had a component-oriented web framework with Ajax-capable components, and there was a port of Lucene to Ruby, I'd be able to build my current projects entirely there. I expect that to happen sometime this year!

Community

The most critical crown jewel for Java is the community. Said another way, Java's market share makes it the 500-lb. gorilla who can sleep anywhere he chooses. Java's community is as massive as it is diverse:

- Vendors across the industry support Java. Though Sun is the inventor, IBM is perhaps the most important Java supporter.
- Enterprise developers use Java to do almost everything. Java is at once a mobile computing platform, a web-based applications language, a systems language for enterprise-plumbing code called *middleware*, and everything in between.

- Hobby programmers flock in droves toward open source projects. Once the black sheep of the open source community, Java has now become the dominant player.

Standards also play a significant role in enterprise computing. From the beginning, the core Java vendors have collaborated to establish standards. Servlets, EJB, and JSP were three of the most influential standards of this decade. To fend off the image that Java was growing increasingly proprietary, they established a community process.

Java has characteristics that many of us take for granted. You can find good Java developers everywhere. No one ever gets fired for choosing Java. It's mature and ready for outsourcing. You can get education. You can buy components. You can often choose between many implementations of a standard. You can do many things for free. I could go on, but the point is clear. Java's community makes enterprise development safe.

The Importance of Open Source

Everyone wants to build a monopoly for the inevitable benefits of market domination, but the power behind Java's community goes well beyond riding the coattails of market leadership. And one piece of the community, open source software, increasingly defines the Java experience.

In the beginning, open source software powered the servlet revolution through Tomcat. Then, we learned to build with Ant, and test with JUnit, and continuously integrate with products like Cruise Control. Later, Struts software changed the way that we organize web-based user interfaces, and Hibernate led a resurgence in transparent persistence. You could easily argue that the most compelling innovations are happening in open source projects, in many areas:

- *Lucene* now provides industrial-strength text-based search.
- *Tapestry* is possibly the most promising successor to Struts.
- *Spring* rather than EJB defines the way that services are applied transparently. With Spring, you can attach declarative services like security, transactions, and remoting to POJOs.
- *Hibernate* is one of the leading providers of transparent persistence.

You can even see the impact of open source software on industry. The EJB 3.0 spec forced vendors to provide a simpler POJO-based API, instead of standing pat and raking in the money from existing EJB 2.x servers. Ant and JUnit changed the evolution of development environments. JBoss created a full open source application server, and is changing the model for software companies.

Now, several companies use the open source community to control certain important technologies. For example, after years of getting hammered in the area of Integrated Development Environments (IDEs), IBM open sourced Eclipse. Now, look at the difference:

- Though IBM spends a fraction of the money on marketing compared to the past, it has an overwhelming lead in market share.
- IBM now has the mind share of the fickle open source community.
- Open source developers contribute eagerly to the Eclipse project, and donate plug-ins for free.
- IBM still maintains some control over the IDE, and more importantly, it keeps its competitors from controlling any aspect of Java through an IDE.

I'm not suggesting that the open source community is easy to manipulate or control. It's a force of its own. If you're starting a new software company or managing a mature one, you have to consider the impact of open source.

Moving Forward

Community played perhaps the key role in the emergence of Java. Without enticing the C++ community, Java would have started much slower, and may never have attracted the support of the core vendors. Without the open source community, many of the innovations that now define Java might never have happened. The challenges for the next major language are daunting.

If there is to be an ultimate challenger for Java, the next successful language will need to achieve a critical mass quickly. That suggests to me that there will need to be some sort of catalyst, like applets in Netscape. The next successful language will probably also need to nurture a massive open source programming community, if it is to enjoy the variety and longevity of Java. Finally, the next language needs to be politically safe (think Ruby, not C#), so standards can emerge without the constant bickering that can get in the way.

Breaking the Myths

As with all technologies that rise so quickly and become so prominent, it's tempting to worship Java. In fact, many media Java proponents use Java's overwhelming success to defend everything from EJBs to static typing. They make a leap of faith to suggest that Java had to be perfect for it to achieve such widespread success. That's dangerous. In fact, many of the following myths may eventually help lead to Java's demise.

Myth 1: Java's Leadership Is Unassailable

Java is indeed in a comfortable position of market dominance. But storms can come quickly. They can destroy the existing landscape, leaving behind a new legacy. Disruptive technologies occur more frequently than you might think:

- Consider the recording industry. Records died, and it looks like CDs may die soon, too. Walkmans rose quickly, and are falling just as fast. A combination of an iPod and a Bose Wave Radio can easily replace a whole stereo in many households.
- Some emerging Third World countries skipped traditional phone systems, in favor of wireless technologies.
- Digital photography has relegated film to a niche product.
- You can't find a 5¼-inch floppy disk anymore, and it's getting harder to find a 3½-inch disk.
- Closer to home, Visual Basic may be nearing the end of its run. Movement to .NET has proven to be disastrous for Microsoft, for the Visual Basic community.

In fact, Microsoft's .NET environment threatens Java *now*. Some emerging programming languages draw the attention of some of Java's brightest independent consultants, and frustrating limitations drive away others. All other programming languages have had a limited period of leadership. In the end, this will be true of Java as well.

Myth 2: Java Is a Great Applications Language

Java didn't succeed because it was the best application programming language. It's not even a particularly good application programming language. Smalltalk and Python are certainly more productive. Visual Basic is simpler. Java succeeded because it was able to grab the existing C++ community, and enable them for the Internet. The community, not the language, represents the most important aspect of Java. Some of the very forces that ushered in the Java revolution may well help lead to its ultimate demise. The C++ legacy, necessary to attract the vast existing community, also limits Java in many ways that we'll explore in Chapter 4.

Beyond the syntax of Java, its explosive success forces Sun to make conservative decisions at the language level. It's doubtful, for example, that we'll see aspect-oriented programming baked into the language, as many think it should be. These decisions, designed to maintain backward compatibility, mean Java simply can't evolve as quickly as its competition. All of this means that Java's evolution is limited, when you compare it to its competition.

Myth 3: Java Is the Most Productive Language

When you compare it to C++, Java is indeed quite productive. That's the cloudy window through which we view Java. But Java's not an application language, any more than C++ was. Anyone who's ever used Basic or Small-talk can tell you about the importance of a rapid feedback loop. Java's compilation requirements and static typing blow away any ability of real-time interpretation or a rapid feedback loop. Static typing is good for preventing some runtime errors, but it's hard on productivity. Java's string handling is limited. Java's syntax lacks features like closures and *code blocks* (which let you pass a block of code as an argument). Again, Java won because it was more productive than the language that most of us were using at the time. It was productive enough. It won't always be.

Corollary 3a: All languages are about the same

Java was able to displace C++ because it offered significant improvements, like garbage collection, a virtual machine, and better OOP. You can often express more with Java in fewer lines of code than you can in C++. The same holds true when you compare Java to some other languages. Languages like Lisp and Haskell offer a higher level of abstraction and a radically different paradigm. Languages like Ruby are far more dynamic, and offer much better access to the building blocks of the language through metaprogramming. Features like code blocks and continuations impact the way you organize and use your libraries, and Java doesn't support either one. In Java, you often have to work much harder to achieve the same result.

Myth 4: Commercial Interests Drive Most Java Innovation

While industry is driving some significant innovation, you could well argue that the most important innovations, like lightweight containers (Spring), web-based application models (Struts and Tapestry), and transparent persistence (Hibernate), are all happening in the open source community right now. These are the ideas that push Java beyond its intended boundaries. In fact, industry goals often hamper rapid innovation:

- It takes time to synchronize massive integrated suites of products. That's why you have to wait so long between releases of WebSphere.

- It takes time to build and test on the scale that's necessary to make big money, in the face of open source competition.
- It takes time to create standards, and more time to adopt them.
- The JCP tries to use the knowledge of experts to invent standards, instead of standardizing inventions born out of experience from successful implementations.

More and more, customers look to open source software to solve critical problems, because they innovate so well. Just as you've witnessed the rise of open source frameworks as a major force, the next popular programming language could well emerge from the open source community.

Myth 5: Big Things Usually Come from Likely Sources

The last few major programming languages have mostly come from unlikely places. The last two didn't even come from major software companies. C came from Bell Labs, a communications company. Java came from Sun, a hardware company. The next popular language will likely come from an unlikely source as well. I don't count C#. It's effectively a Java clone. And the roots of success of Visual Basic came from a small company, operating on a razor-thin budget out of a garage in the Pacific Northwest, called Microsoft.

Java is a mere programming language. Like all languages, its moment in the sun, and its leadership, will prove to be limited. The question is not if, but when.

Looking Ahead

So far, I've tried to paint an accurate picture of Java's success. I owe much of my career to the fathers of Java, and the incredible run of success it's had. Still, I believe that Java is not the unassailable juggernaut that many believe it to be. I think that Java is drifting away from the very developers who made it successful, those who could download a relatively simple language and environment to get an applet or servlet running quickly. Further, some of the very compromises that made Java attractive to the C++ base, like primitives, static typing, and a C++-like syntax, are beginning to work against it. Simply put, Java has reaped the benefits of effective compromises. In the next chapter, we talk about the costs.

CHAPTER 4

Glass Breaking

I don't know for sure when I decided that the kayakers behind us were in trouble. Our minds were occupied by the chaos around us, and the situation kind of snuck up on us. Barton Creek was in flood, and it was pounding furiously. We'd left with 10 paddlers, but needed to keep a safe distance. We divided into groups of three so that each group could keep an eye on the others. The day had already started badly; a fireman in an unrelated party had died on this same stretch of creek. An expert boater had been foolishly paddling alone. Now, we had problems of our own.

After we'd paddled for about an hour, we pulled over into a huge eddy to get the group together and plan our assault on the next dangerous stretch of river. In truth, the banks were very dangerous, with trees that could trap you like a kitchen strainer while the water piled up and poured over you, but the main lines were pretty straightforward. I'd flipped once, but rolled back up easily. But we'd passed a few places that could have given you trouble, had you been unlucky enough to blunder into them, or too cocky to skirt the danger. The last party of three was missing, and we had no way of getting back up the river. We waited for two hours, but the last group of three failed to join us. We waited until there was little daylight left, and then we headed down the river. Eventually, we discovered that one in the trailing party had tried to punch a hole that none of us was brave or stupid enough to run, and had to be rescued by helicopter. I've never run Barton Creek again with water that high.

I've developed a good instinct for trouble on the river, and at work. In this profession, I generally know when a technology smells wrong, or dangerous, and I guide my customers away. I'm sensing that danger around Java right now. It's getting too difficult to manage, and both evolutionary and revolutionary steps to remedy the problem are failing us. In this chapter, I'll introduce some of the basic problems.

Java's New Job Description

So far, I've tried to make the case that Java's always been a generalized programming language, with the syntax and core community coming from the C++ systems language. Also, I've suggested that most early Java applications focused on the user interface. You could download Java and get something running very quickly.

Once Java moved to the server side, it became the core server-side development language. Java carries an increasing load in enterprise development, from object-relational mapping with distributed transactions to messaging with XML binding for service-oriented architectures. So the job that we use Java to do is ever changing. The language is remarkably flexible, so it's lived up to the challenge so far.

But all of the extra power comes with added complexity. Where does that leave people who need to learn a language quickly, or the Java programmer who wants to solve a simple problem, or companies like start-ups that value productivity over all else? As competitive pressures force us to meet shorter and shorter schedules, a generalized Java is just not enough anymore. At some point, Java *will prove* inadequate. Let's look in detail at what we're asking Java to do.

Typical Requirements

If Java dies, I think it will be replaced one niche at a time. Java's popular in several niches. It's floundering in some and thriving in others:

- Java's become indispensable for writing middleware, the systems software that fits between an application and an operating system. Java's many libraries, performance, portability, and ubiquity make it a good fit for middleware, and that's likely to continue.

- For servlets and web programming in general, Java needs a faster feedback cycle, and needs to get better at managing strings. PHP is far more productive for this environment. Java's not the only reason: web programming is a mess for many reasons. But Java just isn't very good for the simplest and most typical applications.

- For XML processing, better alternatives exist. I'd argue that Java's over-reliance on XML is part of the problem, but let me point out that Java is not a particularly good language at handling XML either. XML requires excellent string parsing and manipulation, and Java is just too verbose in this space. Already, the Ruby XML processing libraries, for example, are friendlier than the Java versions, and nearly as fast, for most jobs.

Some other languages have excellent XML support. They will only get better over time.

- For large enterprise projects requiring things like distributed transactions across multiple resources, heavy legacy integration, and code that relies on niche libraries, Java's large libraries and the availability of Java developers make it a natural fit. It will continue to find a role here for quite some time. Be careful, though. Most projects in the enterprise are smaller projects that could benefit from a more productive language.

Instead of looking at the entire Java landscape, let's narrow it down a bit and consider the requirements for the most typical Java job. I'll go out on a limb and suggest that the most common Java job is to take a big, fat relational database and baby-sit it with a web-based user interface. As a consultant, I see variations of this job more often than any other.

I realize that I'm painting Java into a smaller niche than it's currently occupying. I do think there's cause to do so. From the beginning, Java has been a converted systems language. The impressive list of libraries expands that scope, and the broad and deep pool of programmers makes it compelling for large enterprise applications. But Java never really has been a general-purpose applications language, though that's the place that most of us use it today.

The Learning Curve

If you're concentrating on putting a web-based frontend on a relational database, Java framework designers have solved this problem repeatedly for eight years. I've got to admit, Java hasn't gotten much better at this job since the invention of JSP. Take a look at one of the earliest servlet APIs in action:

```
public class HiMom extends HttpServlet {
  public void doGet(HttpServletRequest req, HttpServletResponse res)
     throws ServletException, IOException {
    response.getWriter().println("<HTML>\nHi, Mom\n</HTML>");
  }
}
```

True, this programming style leads to ugly code with nearly impossible maintenance. It couples view logic much too tightly to business logic. But it is very easy to understand. With the first release of Tomcat, after a few minutes of setup and less than 10 lines of code, you could write a "Hello, World" servlet.

Now the same application involves more effort. With the latest release of Tomcat, you can't just write a servlet anymore. You also need to code up a deployment descriptor and package it all up in a standard WAR file. That

means you've got to learn more about Tomcat, more about the servlet specification, and more about XML. As a consequence, the getting-started documentation for Tomcat has grown from a couple of pages to dozens of pages.

You might not think that substantial increases in the learning curve for
Tomcat matter much. You might be willing to make such an investment in
Tomcat, because it's such a core technology. The problem is that it doesn't
stop with the servlet API. You need much more to build a typical Java application today than you needed five years ago:

- You'll likely need to understand Ant, the typical tool that most of us use
  to build and deploy web applications.
- Then, you'll need to understand Tapestry, or Struts, or some other web
  MVC framework, to help you organize your user interface code base.
- Most of us try also to learn an object relational mapper, like Hibernate.
  While it does relieve some of your persistence burdens, it also imposes a
  steep learning curve.
- You'll probably want a framework like Spring to organize your applica-
  tion resources and make this whole strategy testable.
- You'll need some education on how to use these tools to integrate them
  and use them together effectively.

My clients that move to Java from another language just shudder when they
see my recommendation of five weeks of education, which lets them cover
only the fundamentals. Java is no longer an approachable language for them.

Java for the typical application

True, Java has improved some aspects of this problem. If you've got a highly
normalized relational database that doesn't lend itself to an object model
very well, you can map it better today than you could then, because of the
emergence of object relational mappers like Hibernate and JDO. You can
better separate the business logic from the view logic, with Struts and better
emerging alternatives like Tapestry. You can attach services like security and
distributed transactions to any Java object with frameworks like Spring.

But if you really come back to the core problem, a web-based user interface
on a relational database, you have to learn much more to do the job today
than you had to learn five years ago. And you have to work harder to
achieve the same results. Most of the added value deals with corner cases, or
noncentral problems. When all is said and done, these advanced frameworks will drive the Java language away from the base that made it so popular. When that happens, Java will be a niche language for large-scale
enterprise development.

Agile Processes

While the requirements for the typical Java application have remained relatively static, radical changes are transforming the typical process that you might use to build it. While not many Java programmers would say they use agile methods like SCRUM or Extreme Programming, more and more of them are using the core techniques from agile processes:

Simplicity

Agile methods suggest that you should use the simplest thing that will work. Simpler frameworks like Spring now displace complex frameworks like EJBs with increasing regularity.

Automated unit testing

We are in the midst of a testing renaissance, and the JUnit framework and agile processes light the way. At conferences I attend, classes like test-first development garner ever-increasing attendance, and polls to the audience indicate that testing is much more common than it has been.

Shortened iterations

Shorter schedules and the need for better integration of customer feedback shorten product development cycles, and also the smaller iterations within those cycles.

Development processes and Java

Java's community and tools provide excellent support for agile development, but there's a catch. Java is not such a good language for agile development. Java is not the simplest of languages. Nor is it friendly to very short iterations. If these two ideas are not clear to you now, they will be clear by the time you finish this book. Other languages let you move from one change to the next without a cumbersome compile/deploy cycle. Other languages have a more expressive syntax, and other frameworks take you to a higher, more productive level of abstraction.

Even as we begin to understand that Java is not the most agile language, those using other dynamic languages are using agile techniques like automated testing to shield them from the problems related to programmer-friendly type and exception strategies. Java's founders believed that it's always better to catch potential bugs at compile time. They did not consider that features like static typing and a heavy emphasis on checked exceptions come at a cost.

If we were to choose a language based on the development methods that we value today, Java would almost certainly not be our language of choice. As the principles promoted by agile developers become prominent, the Java language will experience increasing pressure.

Basic Java Limitations

I've painted a picture of the average project. The average team builds or ports applications that will deliver a web-based frontend on a relational database, potentially with other less meaningful services. The team probably uses increasingly agile principles, and likely wants to do unit testing. The team typically works under short schedules and great pressures. And given more dynamic alternatives, Java is not at all the language that I'd usually choose for such a project, in such an environment:

- The many frameworks designed to simplify the Java development experience do make experienced Java developers more productive, but make the learning curve too steep for those new to Java.
- Compile-time checking of exception and types adds safety, but comes at a cost of additional time and syntax.
- Java's inability to express structured data leads to an over-reliance on XML, with the corresponding additional complexity and bloat.
- Java's many compromises, like primitives, make Java harder to learn and more complex to write.
- Java is more dynamic than C++, but is nowhere near as dynamic as languages like Smalltalk and Ruby. Java developers are finding metaprogramming, but they're not able to execute on those ideas fast enough.
- Java's long compile/deploy cycle is much longer than interpreted, dynamic alternatives.

Taken alone, none of these issues hurts enough to matter. Taken together, Java becomes much less productive for most developers.

Steve Yegge: Java's Limitations
Language expert and creator of Wyvern

Steve Yegge, a graduate of the University of Washington, spent five years as an Assembly-language programmer at Geoworks and more than six years as a software development manager at Amazon.com. Steve somehow managed to find time to design, implement, and maintain a massive multiplayer game called Wyvern (http://www.cabochon. com/), with a half-million lines of Java and Python code.

What is your experience with Java?

SY: I was a card-carrying member of the Java community from late 1996 through mid-2003. I used Java to build a cool, multiplayer, user-extensible online game. Java got me really far, and I loved it for seven years.

Why did you start looking at other languages?

SY: I simply hit a productivity wall. As my code base grew, my innovation slowed, until finally, tasks were taking me an order of magnitude longer than I felt they should. I stopped development for six months and did a deep-dive investigation to figure out what the heck was going wrong. It wasn't what I expected. The problem was Java. I was pretty unhappy about this. I'd invested an awful lot in Java. AOP helped a little (albeit at a high entry cost), but nowhere near enough. Nothing else helped at all. What I needed was a new language.

How does Java hold you back?

SY: First, Java offers an impoverished set of abstractions. No first-class functions, no reference parameters, no keyword or default params, no destructuring bind or even parallel assignment, no way to return multiple values efficiently, no continuations, no user-defined operators, no generators, no closures, no tuples…the list just goes on. Java's about 25 teeth shy of a full mouth.

Second, Java is entirely nonextensible. It can't grow. There's no metaprogramming, no macros, no templates, nothing that gives you syntactic abstraction. So, Java's incompressible. Java code is always filled with stuff that looks like copy and paste, but you can't factor it out. Java code and APIs always wind up bloated (and yet oddly impressive looking).

Third, Java can express code, but not data. You're stuck using property files, XML, and other means of defining data. But the line between code and data is blurry—think about configuration, for example. So, the Java folks are piling on framework after framework, creating this huge pipeline of transformations that can't be expressed in Java.

Fourth, Java's static type system sucks. Actually, all static type systems suck, but Java's is worse than most. It gives you only narrow avenues along which you're permitted to think. Java programmers must painstakingly learn to pound star-shaped pegs into square holes; this is what design patterns are mostly about.

Fifth, Java has far too much nonessential complexity. For instance, it now has *four* kinds of types: primitives, classes, arrays, and enums. All the type types have their own syntax and semantics, which you must learn and then handle in your APIs. It's not just types, either. Java's entire syntax is large and bureaucratic. Java's syntax is complex for no good reason.

Typing

One of the most fiercely debated topics in programming languages is the benefit of strong, static typing strategies. Java's strategy opts for as much compile-time checking as possible. Let's take a quick overview of programming language design, in layman's terms. Then, you can put Java into context. When building a language, a designer needs to answer two typing questions relatively early in the design process.

Strong Versus Weak Typing

Strong versus weak typing decides how a type is enforced, or interpreted. In a weakly typed language (like C), variables can be coerced easily, or interpreted as something else. A strongly typed language strictly enforces compatible types across operations. It probably doesn't surprise you that Java is a strongly typed language.

Ruby, Smalltalk, and Python also enforce strong typing, which might surprise you. Many developers believe Smalltalk, Python, and Ruby are so productive because they are weakly typed. They are misinformed. Consider this brief Ruby example:

```
irb(main):003:0> i=1
=> 1
irb(main):004:0> puts "Value of i:" + i
TypeError: cannot convert Fixnum into String
        from (irb):4:in `+'
        from (irb):4
```

In the first line, the undeclared variable i takes on the value of 1. At this time, Ruby decides that i is a Fixnum. When Ruby interprets the third line, it sees the + operator after the string, and tries to concatenate i. Of course, Ruby doesn't know how to concatenate an integer to a string, so it throws an error. That's clearly an example of strong typing. (Actually, I've oversimplified things a little. You can dynamically change the definition of Ruby classes and objects at runtime, and this weakens the typing somewhat. Still, on a continuum from strong to weak typing, Ruby would lean slightly to the strong side.)

In a similar situation, a language with weaker typing may instead coerce types to a compatible form, as in C. Consider this example:

```
int a = 5;
float b = a;
```

In the second line, C coerces the value of the integer to float. Other examples are even worse. In C++, the ( ) cast operator does not yield type safety, so you could say, for example:

```
Cat *cat;
Dog *dog = (Dog *)cat;
```

These are legal C++ statements. Instead of reporting an error, C++ will happily go on stomping through memory. Languages with very weak typing simply do not capture typing errors, so the behavior of certain operations is undefined. Weaker typing is sometimes convenient, and less predictable. As you've seen, typing is not always black and white. It's also a highly contentious issue among language experts. Strong versus weak typing is on a continuum. Some strongly typed languages like Java allow loopholes by letting the user cast objects to another type. Languages with the strongest possible typing allow no loopholes. Weaker typing allows, and may even require, coercions. The weakest possible typing doesn't do type checking at all at compile time or runtime, like Assembly language, for example.

Static Versus Dynamic Typing

The more interesting question by far is when typing is enforced. Static typing binds a type to an object, and language constructs like variables and parameters. Dynamic typing binds a type to an object at runtime. Dynamic typing doesn't say anything about a variable's container, or anything that a variable passes through. The type is bound to the object. Therefore, the type of containers can change. An imperfect rule of thumb is that static languages force you to declare variables, but dynamic languages don't.

Ironically, most dynamic languages also tend to be strongly typed. Most weakly typed languages tend to be static. Said another way, strong typing can be dynamic or weak, but weak typing is usually also static. You don't find many weakly and dynamically typed languages, beyond Assembly language. Figure 4-1 places programming languages on two axes. Java has strong, static typing. You know this, because you get type mismatch errors when you make certain kinds of mistakes. Compiling this:

```
class TypeTest {
  public static void main(String args[]) {

    i = 4;                    // Nope!!! Static typing

    int j;
    j = 4.2;                  // Nyet!!! Strong typing
  }
}
```

...gives you this result:

```
TypeTest.java:3: cannot resolve symbol
symbol  : variable i
location: class TypeTest
    i = 4;

TypeTest.java:5: possible loss of precision
found   : double
required: int
    j = 4.2;
```

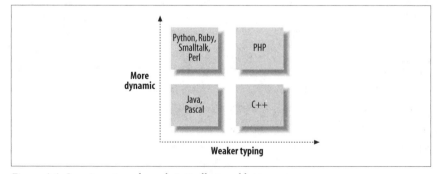

Figure 4-1. Java is a strongly and statically typed language

Sometimes, that's good. After all, a bug that gets caught at compile time takes much less time than a bug that gets solved much later. In general, though, the dynamic programmers that I interviewed said static typing simply mauls productivity.

Syntax

Initially, you immediately can see that Java's syntax forces you to do more work. You have to declare and type all of your variables and parameters. You also need to cast objects that are compatible but different, and convert objects that aren't. The extra syntax provides value—the compiler has more information to catch bugs earlier. There's a cost, too. Static typing makes you work harder to enter equivalent code to dynamically typed languages, but you also have more lines of code to understand, maintain, or enhance. It's very difficult to prove or disprove the notion that static typing makes you more or less productive in terms of hours at the keyboard, but you can show that static typing leads to more characters, and more code to read and maintain.

Raw code count is not definitive; if it were, Perl, with all of the two- or three-character shortcuts, would be the most productive language of all time. Still, it's suggestive. Java's syntax wouldn't be such a problem if you could limit the extra code to a few lines of code at the top or bottom of a program, but you can't. You need to declare types for parameters. You need a cast every time you take something out of a collection. This syntax only gets more invasive with generics.

Thought Process

Some of the costs related to typing are *hidden costs*. I believe that one such cost is related to high-level, conceptual work versus finishing work. It's usually preferable to do conceptual work first and finishing work later, because much of your code will be thrown away, especially at early stages. As your program takes shape, you can do more and more detailed work. You make the expected case work, and then you work through noncritical path issues.

Java forces you to work the opposite way: to make things compile, you must deal comprehensively with typing, which involves dominantly finishing issues. Also, many of the compiler errors in Java might not even be problems at all in a dynamically typed language.

Code/Compile Cycle

Dynamic typing comes into play especially when you need to experiment. Remember, you must declare variables in statically typed languages. In Java, that means you need to start each application with a class definition, and it snowballs. You can't just jump in and evaluate a single line of code—the compiler just doesn't have enough information. Instead of just simply evaluating statements, you need to blow out a class, type everything, compile, and execute. In Smalltalk, Lisp, Basic, and Ruby, you can just start typing. For simple experimentation on an initial cut at a Fibonacci sequence, here's the Java version:

```java
class Fib {
  public static void main (String args[ ]) {
    int x1 = 0;
    int x2 = 1;
    int total = 1;
    for (int i=0; i<10; i++) {
      System.out.println(total);
      total = x1+x2;
      x1 = x2;
      x2 = total;
    }
  }
}
```

It's 13 lines; 41 words; 226 characters. Keep in mind that Java forces you to declare the class to explore, and that's what we're measuring here. On the command line, you need to save, compile, and run. The Ruby counterpart looks like this:

```ruby
x1 = 0
x2 = 1
100.times do
  puts x2
  x1, x2 = x2, x1+x2
end
```

It's 6 lines; 16 words; 57 characters. Notice how the code just flows better. Read it in English. But the biggest impact is on experimentation. You just type and go. You can cut and paste right on the console screen. You'll use command retrieval to repeat the lines that you need. And these advantages come into play in IDEs as well. Further, if you need 100 iterations, the Java version breaks because an int is not big enough. Ruby still works fine.

This is a trivial example, and probably not completely fair. After all, the Java version packages up a full class and the Ruby version doesn't need to. But you'll find that as we go on, the examples get more and more compelling, especially for the dynamic, reflective style of programming that leading Java developers seek today.

As you add the Web and other deployment steps, the case for dynamic languages gets more compelling, because you can make changes and immediately see the results, instead of having to compile and deploy, and maybe even bounce your servlet engine. Web-based programming gets very easy. Just make a change, and hit Reload.

From my small forays into Basic (where I made my spending money in high school by writing games) and Smalltalk (where I did marketing demos), I miss the rapid feedback cycle afforded by dynamic typing and an interpreter the most.

Adaptability

If you've been coding in Java for most of your career, you probably don't know that you have to jump through so many hoops just to support static typing, but you do. One of the greatest typing costs comes into play when you refactor. Think of the impact of a simple type change for a member variable. You've got to change the property, the getters and setters, every type cast, and every parameter usage. Dynamically typed languages delay the binding of a type to a variable or a parameter, so you often don't need to make any change at all to support a simple type change. For Smalltalk, for example, you can change a type easily. If the new type supports all of the messages of the old type, you will likely limit the changes to one place in your code.

Generics

The Java architects have traditionally gone to great lengths to ensure type safety, but there's been one particular case that's troubled them. When you take an object from a collection, you need to cast the object:

```
ArrayList animals = new ArrayList( );
animals.add("elephant");
String cat = (String)animals.get(0);
```

The compiler has just lost the ability to provide compile-time type safety. You could call the array element anything you want. To fix this, Java introduces an ugly implementation of a feature called generics. Here's what the usage looks like:

```
ArrayList<String> animals = new ArrayList<String>( );
animals.add("elephant");
String elephant=animals.get(0);
```

Comparing the preceding code with its nongeneric equivalent, you may think that you avoided casting, but you really did not. Java introduced an ugly implementation of generics, called *type erasure*. Under the hood, in the modified version, the ArrayList still maintains a collection of Objects and not a collection of Strings. Of course, any library that you need to strongly type with user-defined types must enable the code for generics. Enabling generics gets a little ugly. Here's the List declaration from within the Java collections package:

```
public interface List<E> { void add(E x);
Iterator<E> iterator( );
}public interface Iterator<E> {
  E next( );
  boolean hasNext( );
}
```

If you're not a fan of statically typed languages, you don't like the extra type checks that place yet an additional burden on you. Even if you like the idea of generics, you probably don't like the implementation. Generics offer only syntactic sugar and not real runtime protection, because the JVM has no concept of generics. In an article series on agiledeveloper.com,[*] Venkat Subramaniam lays out the problems in gory detail:

- You lose type safety when you mix nongenerics with generics. For example, List notGeneric = genericList; type safety would not flow into notGeneric, even though it's bound to the same list as genericList in memory.

- You can't use primitive types as parametric type or static fields of generic type.

- Instances of different parameterized types (like ArrayList<String> and ArrayList<Book>) belong to the same type ArrayList.

- Since the JVM has no notion of generics, other classes won't be able to take advantage of generics via reflection.

So, if you're protected at only a superficial level, and if new languages can't participate in the solution, the syntax only serves to further burden users with details and inconsistencies, prompting the question, are generics a solution begging for a problem? When I ask my students how many class cast exceptions they get from collections, very few say this is a significant problem.

---

[*] Venkat Subramaniam. Generics in Java, parts 1–3 (June 2005); *http://www.agiledeveloper.com/ articles/GenericsInJavaPartI.pdf, ...GenericsInJavaPartII.pdf, GenericsInJavaPartI.pdf.*

Ted Neward: Generics
Author of *Effective Enterprise Java*

Ted Neward is an independent consultant specializing in high-scale enterprise systems. He is an author, teacher, and consultant, focusing on Java .NET interoperability. He has written several widely recognized books in both the Java and .NET space, including the recently released Effective Enterprise Java (Addison Wesley). He lives in the Seattle area with his wife, two sons, two cats, and eight PCs.

What's wrong with Java, in general?

TN: Hordes of developers are writing code that doesn't fit well with the tools and technologies they're using to build applications, pronouncing the tools and technologies "ugly and unusable" and going off to reinvent the wheel.

What's wrong with Java 1.5?

TN: Java 1.5 demonstrates a general attitude against progress, and Sun adamantly refuses to advance the JVM whatsoever, preferring instead to maintain the fiction that the Java language and the JVM are one tightly coupled entity.

Do you like the implementation of generics?

TN: No. The fact that they're implemented at a language level, rather than at the JVM level, means that under the hood, it's all still just Object references, so:

- Other languages have no concept of generics.
- We get no performance boost from generics.
- We have to have some sneaky backward compatibility that still permits use as Object references (which you might argue would be necessary anyway, and I'll suggest that the Object-reference versions should be deprecated in 1.5 and removed in 1.6).

Overloading

In some ways, Java's typing problems are exacerbated by another limitation described as a feature: method overloading. Taken alone, overloading is not a huge problem, but Java developers use overloading to enable an API that supports multiple types. You've got a surefire recipe for API bloat.

Need an example? Take the java.util.Array interface. Please. For convenience, you get more than 70 methods. Peel back the onion, and you see they cover only 10 or so pieces of actual, distinct functionality. With a smarter method declaration, you'd be able to specify parameters with keywords, and default unused parameters to an intelligent value, like 0 or null.

Other Costs

When you decide to type everything, it's a slippery slope. When you need to pull back from Java's typing system, you can't always do so. You're starting to see many examples of Java libraries working around the typing in unusual ways. Study the JMX interface for an excellent example. Does it use strong typing? It appears that way, at first. Then you dig in a little and find what only can be conceptually described as an embedded type system—a mini-language, embedded in a String parameter called ObjectID, with a complete language description in the JavaDoc and syntax completely opaque to compilers and interface generators and processors. Java's type system *failed* here. JMX architects bypassed the type system, building metadata into strings and other objects. If you look around, you'll find other examples of this as well. Most often, Java hides weaker types, or dynamic types, as strings.

The Benefits of Static Typing

After reading about all of the negatives, you're probably wondering why anyone would ever opt for strong, static typing. There are at least two compelling reasons to do so. Static typing reduces certain types of errors (like misspelled variable names), and provides more information for your IDE and other tools. (Most security-related typing arguments refer to weak typing, not dynamic typing.)

Take the following application. Java will catch this error at compile time:

```
int consumer;
if (conusmer == 0) return consumer;   //spelling error
```

It's hard to imagine a dynamic language, with rigorous unit testing, letting an error like this through, though. The IDE problem is a little bit more obscure. Many of the features that Java developers have come to depend on, like method completion, rely on information in a variable's type. You can't always get the same contextual information out of a Ruby or Smalltalk IDE.

A Safety Net with Holes

The Java founders most often cite the ability to catch type mismatch errors at compile time rather than runtime. That's interesting to me, because of all the Smalltalk and Ruby developers I interviewed, few have ever had significant problems with type mismatch errors. Of course, most of them lean pretty heavily on automated unit testing, as we all should. You need to unit test code regardless of whether you use dynamic typing. No compiler can guess your intent perfectly. Even if you like the generics implementation, you've got to be concerned with an implementation that's little more than syntactic sugar, with no JVM implementation behind it.

With the heavy use of test-driven development, the argument for reduced bugs is much less compelling. In fact, Java's type safety is not as encompassing as the founders would lead you to believe. At any given time, most of the objects in a typical Java application reside in collections. Any time you remove one of these objects from its collection, you need to cast up from Object. You're effectively retyping an object. If you cast it incorrectly, glass will break in the form of a class cast exception, at runtime. At the same time, improved tools and emphasis on automated unit testing make it much easier to catch type problems in dynamic languages long before they ever reach production. My experience tells me that Java's type safety is not as important and comprehensive as most programmers think it is, and the typing in more dynamic languages, with unit testing, is not as limiting.

The IDE code completion problems presented by dynamic typing will probably get solved by a combination of better browsers and smarter context. Unit testing will make type safety less useful from a program correctness standpoint. In the end, for application programming, more dynamic typing will prevail. The productivity gains due to dynamic typing are too compelling to ignore.

Primitives

From the very beginning, Java designers consciously made decisions to attract the C++ community, and favor performance over other considerations. The biggest compromise was the inclusion of primitive types. This addition means Java is not fully object-oriented, and presents several significant challenges. Those who came from the C++ community don't always see a problem, but developers from other programming languages often see primitives as an ugly kludge. Primitive types do not descend from Object, so Java is more of a hybrid language than a true object-oriented language. But that's all academic. There's a real cost associated with the theory.

Primitives Are Limited

Java primitives limit you because they don't descend from a common Java object. One of the nice things about most object-oriented languages is polymorphism: you can deal with specific objects in a general way. In Java, that's not quite true, because primitives do not descend from Object. You can't, for example, say 6.clone( ), or 6.getClass( ).

If you've ever built an XML emitter or an object relational mapper, you know about the headaches related to primitive support. In Java, you can't treat all types the same, and you don't have the benefit of natural methods on the primitive types. You have to build in explicit support for objects, primitives, and arrays.

Since most of us don't build XML emitters or persistence frameworks, we shouldn't care about those costs, right? It's not that easy. You still have to deal with complications in the language, such as inconsistent APIs and added breadth of the frameworks that you do support. Reflection is probably the worst. To get the value of a field, you first have to determine the type. You then get the value, with one of get, getBoolean, getByte, getChar, getDouble, getFloat, getInt, getLong, or getShort. Of course, if it's an array, all bets are off. Arrays can contain primitives or objects, so they can't even treat their contents generically. You basically have to go through the whole process again.

Reflection in pure object-oriented languages is much simpler. To get a field's value, you use a single API to query a field, and get an object back. You can then query the object to find the defining class. If you want to deal with it as a top-level object, you don't even have to do that.

Primitives Are Unnaturally Verbose

Of course, you need to be able to do some things to a primitive that the primitive itself can't do. Java solves this problem by providing type wrappers. Primitives are so awkward because sometimes you use the primitive and sometimes you use the wrapper. It's very difficult to be consistent with usage.

When you add the additional wrappers and casts, you find that primitives don't help make Java cleaner, and they make it only marginally faster. Since you have both types and wrappers, you often need to convert between the two, forcing unnecessary syntax, and often unpredictable behaviors (such as several strange behaviors in the autoboxing in Java 1.5).

The Big Trade-off

All in all, primitives were important in one sense: supporting them let Java aggressively attract C++ developers, because the idea and syntax were similar. In retrospect, though, it's created some significant problems, in terms of language clarity, productivity, and readability.

In retrospect, we're paying for the early compromises that it took to draw away the C++ community. That's a fair trade, in my book. Don't underestimate the cost, though. Primitives complicate the code base, lead to inconsistencies, and bloat the language. The next popular programming language will probably not be a hybrid language, with both objects and primitives. C++ started the transition to object-oriented programming and Java finished it. We don't need a crutch anymore.

Parting Shots

Of course, you could write a whole book about the strengths and weaknesses of Java alone. I don't think that's productive. I won't rehash the "EJBs stink" message that's been presented prominently in my last three books. I also don't want to launch into a debate about the meaning of whitespace, Java's commenting styles, or the relative benefits or evils of byte code enhancement. Still, there are more things to cover. Exceptions and strings play a huge role in most Java applications.

Sun

Sun is not the company that it once was, placing Java's future in doubt. I'm not saying that Java will disappear, but Sun might. It has lots of cash in the bank, but where is it going to make money? It's being squeezed on the low end by companies like Intel, Dell, and AMD. IBM is squeezing Sun from above. Sun's software and services businesses have never really taken off. I think Sun is a ripe acquisition target.

If Sun does have major problems, what happens to Java? I fear that an IBM acquisition would put too much emphasis on the hardest enterprise problems, moving Java further away from its base. Open sourcing Java could effectively splinter the language. Other potential suitors, like Oracle and BEA, could lead to a conflict of interest that could stymie new standards.

IBM may be getting nervous. It has begun to hedge its Java position in several ways:

- IBM is aligning closely with BEA on standards like SDO, and it is increasingly at odds with the JCP. IBM may well be positioning itself to challenge the JCP, or establish standards outside of the JCP.
- IBM looks like it may embrace PHP more closely, to take advantage of that swelling marketplace. PHP would be an effective hedge for smaller and intermediate businesses.
- IBM continues to invest in XML technologies with Microsoft.

In any event, Sun's ultimate health, or lack thereof, casts doubt on the shape of Java's future. If you're trying to maintain market dominance, uncertainty is not the best place to start.

Exceptions

Like static typing, Java's emphasis on checked exceptions seems like it's on unshakable footing. The argument goes something like this: if a typical developer doesn't have to deal with an exception explicitly, he probably won't deal with it at all. For me, and for many of my customers, checked exceptions tend to hurt more than they help, for many reasons:

- The exception syntax is incredibly invasive. Exceptions easily dominate a typical method, even at very low levels, when you can't do anything about them.

- Most of the time, you can't deal with an exception, so you can only throw it up the chain anyway. You shouldn't have to do a job explicitly that the compiler can do for you.

- Having so much exception syntax deadens you to the few lines of exception code that actually do something important. Said another way, it's hard to see the diamond through all the mud.

Recently, Java frameworks like Spring and AspectJ have begun to recognize the power of unchecked exceptions. Hibernate founder Gavin King has often said that he would have built Hibernate on an unchecked exception model if he had a chance to do it over again. Hibernate converted to unchecked exceptions at Version 3.

Expressing Data

Programming and data go hand in hand. In most other languages, structured data becomes a natural part of an application. Part of Java's over-reliance on XML comes from its limited ability to express structured data. In Ruby, I can quickly declare a hash map of arrays, for example. Such structures dramatically ease configuration and allow natural metaprogramming.

Strings

If you look at Perl, you can quickly understand what it's designed to do. It's a turbo-charged text manipulation engine. Though it's very complicated in other ways, Perl has been so popular because it does what it's designed to do.

By contrast, if you look at Java, you don't have the same convenient, high-powered text manipulation. That's surprising, especially when you look at the core job that we ask Java to do. Servlets, XML, JSP, HTML, and many other constructs are strings. In fact, I probably work with strings in some form more often than I do anything else. It's amazing to me that Java's not any better than it is when it comes to strings. Its pattern-matching support is second class, and the major string APIs are at an extremely low level.

Simplicity

Java's already a good language for big, hard-core enterprise programming projects. It's getting better at solving that problem. And Java's never been good at tiny applications that you might write for a small business in Visual Basic. There's a huge middle ground between these two problems. Java stepped into this gap with a vengeance and ripped the heart out of Microsoft's enterprise programming community. But Figure 4-2 shows Java is leaving that community behind rapidly.

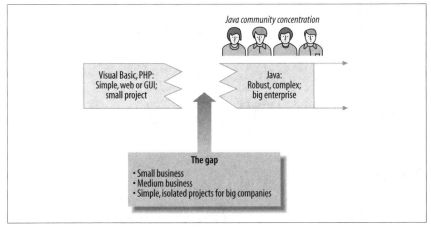

Figure 4-2. Java has controlled the gap between enterprise projects and small ones, but is now leaving that community behind

In my past three books, I've made the case that Java has to get simpler to thrive. That's not happening. Java's power structure is entrenched firmly in the enterprise space. In the past three Java One conferences, Sun has paid lip service to the need to simplify the Java API, but we're seeing only limited focus on richer user interfaces. The big vendors claim a drive to simplification, but the ultimate answer is EJB 3.0, generics, and Java Server Faces (JSF).

In fact, Java is moving away from its base. Remember, huge numbers of us are waiting for better, simpler ways to baby-sit a relational database with a web frontend. Instead, we're seeing more XML, more configuration, more layers of abstraction, and a steady drift away from the user interface and the end user. Java takes longer to learn and is no longer approachable.

Tools

One of the symptoms to this problem is Java's over-reliance on tools. We Java developers love our IDEs. The truth is that we can't live without them. In the not-too-distant past, I did some research for a major application server vendor. I found that the most productive developers liked the command line better. You can always find a command line, and an editor. If you're comfortable with these tools, you can go anywhere.

But in the past three years, we reached a tipping point of sorts. The smartest developers are moving toward IDEs, because the language has become too complex to manage without them. You simply need an IDE to do any real degree of refactoring. Other languages have IDEs, and also good programmers who are very comfortable without them.

Why Not Just Fix Java?

You might argue that we need to fix Java, not scrap it. That would be easy if you could pinpoint the problems. If you thought the problems were in the language itself, you could just do some major surgery and offer a new version of Java. That's easier said than done. Sun has been very careful to preserve backward compatibility at all costs. If you look at the lack of commercial acceptance for Visual Basic .NET, it's easier to respect Sun's point of view. Microsoft made some radical changes to the language and libraries, and they weren't well received. Regardless of whether it's a good idea, Sun will continue to be conservative to protect customers.

Still, even if you look at relatively aggressive changes, most experts that I interviewed tend to think Sun is even now moving in the wrong direction. Instead of making Java more nimble and dynamic at the foundation, the changes, for the most part, amount to additional type safety—syntactic sugar hacks built into the syntax rather than the JVM that often lead to inconsistent behavior.

Libraries and Community

It's clear that libraries are problems, too. Sun has launched several belated simplification movements. So, if it's Java's libraries that are broken, and not the language itself, couldn't we just scrap a few libraries and start over on a more simplified foundation? That's the approach we suggested in *Better,*

Faster, Lighter Java. For Java's most important and basic job, a web-based user interface on a relational database, I don't think Java's frameworks are moving in a healthy direction at all. Most frameworks are moving to add more compelling features rapidly, instead of simplifying what's already out there.

One bad library might point to a few local mistakes. Java's problems are more global. They target very complex problems at the expense of the easy problems that most Java developers need to solve. The problem is clear. The Java leadership is abandoning its base willingly and rapidly. It's a cultural problem, inherent in the Java community, vendors, programmers, and leadership. Java has become strictly a language for hard-core enterprise development of large-scale problems.

Alternatives

Over the next five years or so, the question in play will be this: are the Java community and expansive code library base worth sacrificing the productivity that other alternatives will bring to bear? So far, the answer has been a resounding "Yes." But we're nearing a point of no return. Java needs radical changes if it wants to continue to be all things to all people, but the community, culture, and leadership behind Java have never produced the kind of structural, sweeping changes that we need. Sun has always treated Java conservatively. The community process has always built the kind of software you'd imagine a community process would build: bloated compromises that please no one in the end. The Java community has always tolerated too much architecture, too much XML, and too many layers.

In the second half of this book, I make the case that a clean, dynamic language could gain footing easily in the gap between Visual Basic and enterprise Java. Once entrenched, it could take the same path Java did, into the enterprise. After all, the lion's share of Java development, even in the enterprise, is not full of distributed transaction and backbreaking loads. Five years ago, most developers that I talked to on a regular basis wanted a good way to baby-sit a big, fat relational database with a web-based user interface. Five years later, they want the same thing.

So far, I've shown you how Java is drifting away from its base. In the next chapter, you'll see the rules of the game for the next major successful language. In the next half of the book, I'll explore what alternative languages have to offer, and whether that will be enough to take you beyond Java.

CHAPTER 5

Rules of the Game

In 10 years of relatively heavy kayaking, a few scary rapids stand out. The Chatooga River had many such rapids. Bull Sluice on the Chatooga had a waterfall pouring through a hole in the riverbed. It was large enough on one end to admit a kayaker, but not big enough to let him back out. Cork Screw had a violent approach and a keeper hydraulic. Woodall Shoals was a placid-looking drop that masked a near perfect hydraulic that I considered unrunnable in my peak paddling years. On such rapids, the margin of error was frighteningly small. You walked around, hit your intended line, or risked getting hurt or dying. Those were the rules of the game.

Let's assume for a moment that you agree with the premise I laid out at the beginning of the book: conditions are ripe for an alternative applications programming language to emerge, because Java is abandoning its base. I'm not going to pretend to know what's next. Hopefully, I'll lay out some interesting languages and frameworks that have promise. I'll also rule out some languages right off the bat, based on the rules of the game.

If you think about it, *you* instinctively know that some programming languages will definitely not be the next big one. Lisp is productive, but the average Joe can't understand it. Perl is rich and powerful, but it's subtly inconsistent, and is prone to produce unmaintainable code. With a little vision and experience, you can apply a similar kind of reasoning to understand the types of languages that might follow Java. I suggest that we define success loosely: the language should be recognized widely and adopted broadly among developers who now use Java. This chapter, then, suggests the characteristics that the language should have to have broad commercial success.

Java Raises the Bar

Each new language is subject to the rules of its time. If you think about new inventions in the world of music, you'll see the same principle in play. Early in the recording industry, a record label would sign an artist to a specified contract, manufacture records, promote them on the radio, and distribute them in stores. You find some of those features today, like many of the roles in the production cycle and the importance of airtime (on radio, and now TV and the Internet). Changes in standards force the industry to retool. Some are relatively minor—changes in record speeds simply forced manufacturers to add capability to record players and recording equipment. Others will almost certainly be more radical. These changes require a critical mass to take hold—CDs achieved a critical mass, but eight-tracks did not. Sometimes, disruptive changes completely redefine the organization and very fiber of an industry. Our kids are redefining the way music is distributed through services like Napster and iTunes. Some artists are distributing their music entirely over the Internet, and they are cutting the publishing industry out of the equation altogether.

New programming languages work in much the same way. Every language leaves behind a legacy. Sometimes, changing languages embrace the legacy. For example, you compiled your C programs into a DLL or an executable. You could take advantage of your C code from C++ by buying a new compiler. You could even use C++ to write procedural code or object-oriented code. C++ changed the way we think, but it did not change much of the machinery. The C programming language was also disruptive in many ways. Java, too, was disruptive, redefining the rules of the game.

Kids like to be able to download songs like "Macarena" instantly, so the old music stores aren't cutting it anymore, and they are closing their doors. Don't even try to open one, unless you plan to bankroll it with your own money. By the same token, we like the convenience of the JVM, the massive open source community, and the focus on the Internet, leaving a higher standard for the next major applications language.

Portability

Remember our technical crown jewels. Java commercially introduced the concept of a virtual machine. It redefined the landscape. You compile Java into intermediate byte code that runs in a virtual machine. We've now gotten a real taste of the advantages of the virtual machine. The next major applications language will almost certainly support a virtual machine. You just can't ignore the benefits:

Security
    If you can secure the virtual machine, it's much easier to secure the language.

Portability

The virtual machine provides a common, clean foundation for the language.

Extensibility

If your language turns out to be inadequate, you can always change the byte code. Java extensions like JDO (transparent persistence) and AspectJ use byte code enhancement to extend the Java language effectively.

Interoperability

Lower-level byte code makes it possible for one language to use the same deployment infrastructure, and even run side by side with other languages.

So, the virtual machine is important. I'll go one step stronger. The next commercially successful language should have a version that runs in the JVM. That would help a language overcome many obstacles, both political and technical.

Dion Almaer: Why Java Will Be Hard to Replace

Dion Almaer is the founder and CTO of Adigio, Inc. He is an architect, mentor, pragmatic, and evangelist of technologies such as J2EE, JDO, AOP, and Groovy. He is the former editor-in-chief of TheServerSide. com J2EE Community and is a member of the Java Community Process, where he participates on various expert groups.

You've been a Ruby on Rails proponent. Do you see Ruby as a potential replacement for Java?

DA: As much as I like technologies such as Ruby, I am skeptical as to how to get them used in the mainstream. There is *too much power* behind the Big Two VMs (JVM/CLR).

"You are saying I should bet my Fortune 500 enterprise on a Japanese Mormon named Matz?"

What are the big obstacles?

DA: Inertia is a serious concern for large companies. What is the roadmap for Ruby? Where are the standards? What is the quality of the various modules? How is Ruby on the mobile phone?....

How might it overcome those obstacles?

DA: Ruby is a top language with some amazing frameworks on top of it, but to get to the next level there probably needs to be more. I would love to see JRuby and Ruby.NET really take off. The bulk of the arguments are political, but they are still very valid.

There are many great things written on top of the JVM. Ruby *feels* best for me as a language (for certain tasks), but the platform is harder to sell. If I can get a merger of the two, I am off to the races. This is why Groovy had promise and Java guys were excited. The language would be "Java" to their bosses, but they could do scripting in Groovy on the side.

There is *a lot* of legacy code out there, so it can be hard to migrate to a different platform right now, unless there is a true migration plan.

Something like Ruby needs its "killer app." Many think it is Rails, but is that enough? What type of projects will be run on Rails? I guess we will see. Don't get me wrong, most of my thinking has been because I *want* the industry to move to languages that are more dynamic. I think we need to…but I am skeptical.

Internet Focus

Java set a new bar for Internet integration, and Java's users took full advantage. Corporations use the Internet internally to discriminate information and control the deployment costs of an application. Businesses use the Internet externally to reach their customers and partners. Enabling applications for the Internet has become the most important problem that a business solves, except maybe database integration. Java enabled a whole new generation of Internet applications, with the servlet programming model, JSP as a compiled template language, and a whole suite of enterprise libraries. The next successful language will have to do the Internet, and do it better than Java.

The Internet has at least two dimensions: interfaces for computers, and interfaces for people. For people, the next language should build more powerful interfaces faster than you can build them in Java. I don't think it's enough to just build simple HTML. You need to be able to build a page that can preserve a common layered look and feel throughout an enterprise, so the next language will need to support some kind of component model. Also, users are just beginning to understand that HTML is not enough. Applications like Google Maps and Google Mail stretch HTML and JavaScript to new levels. That's going to be very important to the next successful language.

In fact, many of the consultants I interviewed for this book believe that HTML is broken in fundamental ways. A broadly successful new language could conceivably present a higher abstraction that makes it easier for the industry to retool, piecemeal. Ruby on Rails and Ajax technologies both seem to be moving in this direction.

Interoperability

Bridging from Java to an emerging language will also be important. Of course, if the new language embraces the JVM, interop at lower levels will not be a problem. Interop on the Internet will undoubtedly play a critical role. I think that leads to three important capabilities: XML, web services, and service-oriented architectures.

XML and structured data

Programming has always meant working with data, yet Java doesn't let you declare nested structured data very well. In Java, you see a proliferation of XML, even where it offers little tangible value. For example, metaprogramming and all kinds of configuration require you to express structured data. The next language should let you declare and express structured data, cleanly and natively.

Still, structured data and a language to describe it are important. If you're dealing with structured data on the Internet, you're probably dealing with XML. The next successful language should let you deal with XML productively, and with good performance. In Java, we've dealt with that problem using parsing schemes, query languages, and binding frameworks. A parser cracks open XML and lets you break it into its constituent parts. A binding framework lets you take an object model and convert it directly to XML, or deal with XML as if it were a native object model. XML query languages like XQuery can reach into a complex XML document to retrieve one named piece of data. It's reasonable to expect an emerging language to support all three XML technologies, and most of them do, to various degrees.

Service-oriented architecture (SOA)

A common structured data format is not enough to bridge two languages. You also need a communications mechanism. One trend in languages like Java is to build loosely coupled services, available on the network, and let them communicate with simple messages, with an XML payload. It's a good strategy for interop, for many reasons:

- SOA works best with coarse-grained architectures, or calling big chunks of code. Interop between languages is a coarse-grained problem.
- SOA is hot. Since it's politically popular, support and mindshare will likely remain high.

- SOA uses Internet standards. That means you can leverage existing infrastructure, like security and existing message protocols.

I'm not sure that web services, as defined by IBM or Microsoft, has staying power. I do believe that a lighter form of web services, called REST, may last. REST stands for Representational State Transfer, and it promotes using services the way Internet sites have used them for years. Like the Internet, REST views the network as a collection of resources rather than a collection of methods (like CORBA or traditional web services.)

A REST-based resource returns a representation of itself, usually in XML form. REST allows and even encourages links. REST-based services are based on well-understood, mature APIs, so unlike the fragile traditional web services stacks, they integrate well with other technologies. They can also rely on existing infrastructure to cache content, build links, or secure communication. It's a powerful paradigm shift.

So, Java provides the first set of rules, shown in Table 5-1. If you want to run this river, you'll need to meet the improved standards set by Java. To do anything less means death.

Table 5-1. Java's legacy requirements

Rule	Description
JVM and/or Microsoft Common Language Runtime (CLR)	Run in the JVM, or at a bare minimum, run in its own virtual machine.
Internet focus	Enable Internet applications.
Internet user interfaces	Allow richer Internet user interfaces.
Service layer	Provide an SOA-style integration with Java.
Web services	Allow some type of web service, whether it's the full web services stack or REST-based web services.
XML	Provide a rich, productive XML API.

Enterprise Integration

In some ways, C redefined enterprise integration, by allowing strong database connectivity across an open API (ODBC for Microsoft applications) and providing transaction monitors like Tuxedo and Encina. C was disruptive—it introduced enterprise programming beyond mainframes. Java continued this legacy with frameworks for transactions, rich database integration, messaging, and many other forms of plumbing code called middleware.

I don't think the next major applications language will initially have to have the full enterprise capabilities of C or Java to succeed. Visual Basic certainly achieved tremendous success without these capabilities by leveraging the services provided by other frameworks written in lower-level languages like C. We've already determined that the next language should interoperate with other Java programs, hopefully within the same virtual machine. It should also interoperate through a coarse-grained service layer. That said, some enterprise capabilities will be very important.

Database Integration

Minimally, a new language should access relational databases in a natural, productive way. I don't think any particular application style is important—you can see wildly successful environments with different strategies:

- Microsoft builds a framework that leverages the power of SQL, row sets, and relational databases. The center of the Microsoft universe, from a data perspective, is the relational database. The strategy can scale very well and is surprisingly productive.

- Java, instead, seems to be moving toward ORM. The center of Java's data universe is an object-oriented, persistent model. Other Java applications leverage JDBC with helper frameworks quite successfully.

- Ruby on Rails takes an intermediate approach. Rails wraps a database table with objects that discover the structure of the database dynamically.

All strategies have strengths and weaknesses, and each could serve as an effective foundation for a new language. I do think that emerging languages, and the core frameworks they need, should try to follow these rules:

Embrace the relational database
  While a language may integrate with alternatives, the relational database should be a first-class citizen. Too much focus on object-oriented databases proved to be a problem for adoption for some Smalltalk frameworks. Object-oriented databases are an elegant solution that ignores the current political realities.

Don't force structure on the relational database
  At some level, a language must make it easy to use existing relational schemas, as they exist. Forcing a surrogate unique identifier rather than a composite primary key also ignores existing realities.

Perform, and scale
  High database performance is the single most important indicator of good application performance.

Transactions and Security

Enterprise developers need the ability to define a business transaction. It doesn't matter how fast you can build incorrect applications. If Joe Bob loses

$50 in an Internet transaction because Sally Sue crashed the server by tripping on a power cord, the framework is not going to make it in the enterprise.

Security is also important, though you could probably argue over how important it could possibly be with the gaping holes in operating system security today. Java has set a bar that's going to be pretty hard to clear in this area. The next big language will need the ability to integrate with existing enterprise security frameworks, at least the Internet-based schemes and standardized ones like LDAP. Table 5-2 summarizes the enterprise features a new language will need.

Table 5-2. Enterprise requirements for a new language

Rule	Description
Database access API	Provide a clean, productive API for database access.
Relational databases	Focus on relational databases first.
Database performance	Database interactions should be very fast.
Transactions	Enable application transaction demarcation.
Language security	Provide a clean foundation for language security.
Application security	Let developers secure their applications.
Security integration	Let developers integrate enterprise security, especially for Internet applications.

Like the Java features, having these basic enterprise features does not guarantee success. They just let you play the game.

Generating the Buzz

Many languages have trumped Java technically, but they still failed. Betamax, too, was technically better than VHS. The biggest factor of the equation is social. Without a credible community, there can be no success. To a programmer, a language is an investment in a future, and even an identity. Call it marketing, or buzz, or even hype. If it's hip, or at least interesting, a language stands a fighting chance. If not, there's no chance at all. In some ways, Java helped pave the way for the next language:

- Communities like TheServerSide and Slashdot provide a forum for new ideas to spread quickly through the Java and non-Java programming communities. It's much easier for smaller projects to create a big buzz.

- The increased emphasis on open source software, partially driven by Java, makes it easier to wrestle control away from larger companies. Also, those same companies find open source technologies easier and less threatening to adopt.

- Many Java standards like Web Services (and lightweight HTTP alternatives) make it much easier to interoperate between languages.

- The JVM will run other languages. A new language on the JVM is a much easier sell than a new language in a new environment.

Still, the challenges of establishing a community are daunting. Microsoft has spent millions of dollars promoting the .NET environment, and the adoption on the server side is still nowhere near Java's adoption, though many of the features and capabilities are similar or superior to Java. Sun, for all of its success with the Java platform, has not been able to capitalize on it in the software realm. Adoption of Sun application servers and management software has been spotty at best. IBM lost the battle of the operating system because it couldn't market a technically superior OS/2.

Programmers are a schizophrenic lot. One moment, we're the ultimate skeptics, ditching the safety of the Microsoft Windows environment for unpredictable Linux systems on our desktops. The next, we're lemmings, adopting hideous architectures like EJB without the slightest bit of proof. You also have many different niches within the programming community. Java's been successful for enterprise developers, but hard-core hackers in the Perl and Python communities frown on Java. And Microsoft developers form cultures all their own, with subcultures in it that favor C++ or Visual Basic.

That means the winning formula will also change. At one point, a dominant personality like Steve Jobs may make the difference, and the next, like with the star-crossed NextStep platform, it's not enough. This is all to say that generating buzz is more art than science, and maybe more luck than art. Still, certain themes and trends ring true.

Open Source

Unless it's a disruptive technology, it's hard to imagine the next major programming language coming from a larger commercial vendor. There's just too much fear and distrust among the major players: Microsoft, IBM, and Sun. Instead, I think a credible alternative is much more likely to emerge from the open source community. The open source model provides a stage for thousands of projects, where they can succeed or fail based on their merits. Projects need to prove effective technologies and marketing amid a cynical, critical audience to succeed. There are several interesting test cases in the open source community now: Perl, PHP, Python, Ruby, and many others. You see far fewer commercial languages with any degree of momentum. The biggest, C#, is effectively a Java clone.

Open source software has something else going for it. Since open source projects usually have no formal support, the community must support the language. This environment tests the community dynamics for a language as well as the technology. Communities take on a personality, like snobbish, edgy, nurturing, or bickering. Larger languages like Java may have subcommunities with personalities all their own. When a language gets sudden attention, the personality of the community will either attract or repel new users. Fine-tuning community dynamics is a difficult proposition, because this personality may be hard to judge from the inside. A new language will need an attractive community to succeed, and the open source community seems like a natural place for that to form.

Economics

While open source frameworks usually lend a certain intellectual honesty to a project, commercial forces will have the deciding vote. A new language needs a supporting ecosystem to thrive, and that means someone has to write a check eventually. Simply put, you can't move away from Java without economic justification. To me, the leading potential economic catalyst is clear—an overwhelming advantage in productivity.

When I stepped away from Java for the first time, I needed an economic mother bird to nudge me out of the nest. Java's just too safe and too comfortable otherwise. Recall that as I write this book, I am calling the shots for a start-up. We're writing a Java application to help engineers configure equipment that measures safety systems in manufacturing plants. I recommended moving the application from Java to Ruby midstream because I found the difference in productivity between the environments too great to ignore. Further, when all was said and done, the new application was easier to maintain with fewer lines of code, it was fast enough, easier to tune, and easier to extend with security. I'd estimate that we're three to five times more productive in Ruby. Certainly, Ruby is not the only language that's more productive than Java, but it's an interesting test case. You'll see more in Chapter 7. Productivity will be the economic catalyst that begins to chip away from the Java base. Productivity will drive the emergence of the next great language.

Approachability

When you look at early adoption for all major successful languages, one of the key issues is approachability. New languages need to grab new users quickly. You should be able to get started quickly, and solve a problem that's important to you immediately. C was approachable because it let hard-core systems programmers solve low-level problems in a high-level language, with much better performance and flexibility than other high-level languages. C++ was approachable because you could write C without modifications, and upgrade to C++ features as you wanted to include them in your programs. Java was approachable because it had a familiar syntax, a friendlier memory model, and a clear, consistent path to Internet solutions. Smalltalk was not approachable, because vendors charged too much—it was too expensive to play.

Though nothing simple has a C++-like syntax, I still think that many languages are approachable because of their friendly, productive syntax with a familiar object model. Python versus Ruby is a good example of differences in approachability. Ruby has one of the most highly productive web environments, and a community and philosophy focused on getting programmers off of the ground quickly and painlessly. You can install components easily, often with two or three words, using a feature called Gems that does the work for you, provided you have an Internet connection. Python, on the other hand, has a simple language and syntax, but the web libraries are nowhere near as approachable. When you start to learn one of them, you don't find the ready tutorials or community reaching out to help you. The Ruby on Rails people understand how to make Rails approachable.

The Killer App

Without some kind of catalyst, it's difficult to imagine how a successful community ever gets started. Applets let Java spread to many desktops quickly. Developers could embed dynamic content into their web pages in a matter of hours.

On the surface, it seems like a language must have a vibrant community to ever get rich enough to succeed on any scale, but the community usually won't come until the language is rich enough. A killer app to a developer is a solution that is so compelling that it transcends language. It alone can rapidly drive community growth. It's not the only way a language can succeed, but it's certainly the most likely way.

The killer app is a popular notion of a catalyst. A killer app solves an important problem in such a forceful way that users are compelled migrate. Think California gold rush. People often point to the Lotus 1-2-3 spreadsheet as the killer app that moved businesspeople to Microsoft Windows. Meanwhile, the killer app for OS/2 never came. For Java, you could easily argue that Netscape made it all possible by putting Java on the desktop of millions of potential developers. Applets, or the idea of deploying applications in a browser, also played a significant role, and it's that concept that morphed into servlets and server-side Java programming. The killer app is a seductive idea, because it encapsulates so many important concepts:

- The catalyst, with economic justification, often takes the form of a killer app.
- Once a solution is technically viable, a killer app enables a rapid growth to critical mass. It often solves a chicken and egg problem: you can't build a sufficiently robust language without community, and you can't build a community without a successful language.
- The killer app often initiates the hype that's required to escape a niche. With the newly found hype, the language can explode from a small, focused niche to a more generally successful language.

Remember, a language alone is rarely enough. Right now, several interesting technologies could possibly grow into potential killer apps. Smalltalk's continuation servers, Ruby's metaprogramming environments, and PHP's many applications like bulletin boards may serve as potential killer apps. We'll look at some potential killer apps in Chapters 7 and 8.

Table 5-3 lists community-centric roles. Each of them will come into play when it's time to determine the next major language.

Table 5-3. Community-centric roles

Rule	Description
Open source	Have a rich open source community.
Productivity	Be much more productive than Java for the simplest commercial applications.
Catalyst	Have a tremendously popular application or framework that transcends programming languages.
Familiarity	Be easy for Java developers to learn.
Simplicity	Make it easy to solve simple problems.

Language Features

It's strange to be more than halfway through the characteristics of the next great programming language without even talking about the major features of that language. When you look at the history of programming languages, it makes more sense. The features of a language are important characteristics for success, but only rarely are they the most important characteristics. Said another way, market share and mindshare matter more than how you interpret whitespace.

Dynamic Typing

Java purists defend strong, static typing with the fervor of English soccer fans. To be sure, static typing does have its advantages:

- Static typing enforces typing rules at compile time, when they are least expensive to fix.

- Static interfaces make it easier to enforce a protocol across important boundaries. For example, systems designers may want to force certain types for C interfaces, or certain remote procedure calls.

- Static typing catches some types of subtle errors at compile time, like the misspelling of a variable name.

Still, as you learned in Chapter 4, there's a related cost, usually in productivity. Java developers often make the comment that you can pay now or pay later. That's strange, because Smalltalk and Ruby programmers rarely make lasting errors related to incorrect typing. Further, disciplined automated unit tests easily catch most type mismatch problems. You've got to unit test your code whether you want to or not, because no compiler can completely guess your intent.

Most Java developers who tout the benefits of strong, static typing fail also to count the cost. When you're learning or playing with a language, the cost is excessive, because you have to declare everything, including a wrapping class, and learn a whole new level of detail. Here's a "Hello, World" example in Ruby:

```
puts "Hello, world."
```

And here's the Java counterpart:

```
class HelloWorld {
  public static void main(String[ ] args) {
    System.out.println("Hello World!")
  }
}
```

A Java program requires a rigidly typed class with a `Main` method. The barrier to exploring in Java is simply much higher. Most of the experts that I interviewed for this book recognized that static typing limits productivity for application development dramatically, though some said they were willing to pay the cost for certain types of code, like systems code and middleware. I think it's fair to assume that for applications development, productivity is important enough to warrant dynamic typing for Java's ultimate successor.

Code Blocks and Continuations

The Java open source community now uses anonymous inner classes with greater and greater regularity. When you need lightweight callback-style functionality, in Java the best way is the anonymous inner class. Here's an example of JDBC-style access in Spring, with the anonymous inner class:

```
JdbcTemplate template = new JdbcTemplate(dataSource);
final List names = new LinkedList( );

template.query("SELECT USER.NAME FROM USER", new RowCallbackHandler( ) {
    public void processRow(ResultSet rs)  throws SQLException {
        names.add(rs.getString(1));
    }
  }
);
```

Here's a code block in Ruby:

```
dbh.select_all("SELECT name, category FROM animal") do |row|
  names << row[0]
end
```

This code example executes the code in bold for each row in the result set, which is passed into the code block's row variable.

For application programming, code blocks show up frequently. Any time you need to iterate through a collection, or a result set, or a file, code blocks come into play. Keeping them simple saves you a tremendous amount of work.

Continuations will also be important. In Chapter 8, you will see how continuations dramatically improve productivity in web-based programming.

Rapid Feedback Loop

Think of a feedback loop as the time between making a change and seeing the impact in running code. New application development principles, like test-first development, work best with a fast feedback loop. Small changes in the feedback loop can make huge differences in overall productivity, because you do it so many times every day. With Java, you need to deal with at least a compile step, and you often add steps for code generation (XDoclet), byte code enhancement (JDO), and deployment (servlets and EJB). For Java, that means you must wait to see a source code change realized in executed code. Developers tend to underestimate the benefits of a small feedback loop, unless they're regularly using a dynamic language and need to go back to a static language.

Smalltalk, Lisp, Perl, Ruby, and Basic all have rapid feedback loops, and they're also incredibly productive languages. C, C++, and Java don't. In fact, Java might not have succeeded if its users had come from a dynamic language supporting a rapid feedback loop.

User Interface Focus

More and more, I'm seeing experts that need to do significant user interface development move away from Java. Given the strong server-side focus of the past six years, that news should not shock any of us. Still, the number of Swing experts who vehemently defend it, without trying a meaningful alternative, confuses me, like two *Titanic* passengers arguing over which deck is prettier as the ship sinks around them. James Duncan Davidson said it best: "Friends don't let friends Swing." User interface development demands more than Java has to give. For most application developers, the framework should do much more for you.

Dynamic Class Model

The Java successor should be much more dynamic, and reflective. Java's reflection API is particularly hostile because it must deal with primitives, arrays, and classes. Let's look at a Java example of reflection. Here's a simple XML emitter provided by Stuart Dabbs Halloway, courtesy of Develop-Mentor:

```
public static void doObject(Object obj) throws Exception {
  Class cls = obj.getClass();
  emitXMLHeader(cls);
  Field[] fields = cls.getDeclaredFields();
  for (int i=0; i < fields.length; i++) {
    Field field = fields[i];
      field.setAccessible(true);
      Object subObj = field.get(obj);

    if (!Modifier.isStatic(field.getModifiers())) {
      if ((field.getType().isPrimitive()) ||
        ((field.getType().getNamxe() == "java.lang.String"))) {
        emitXML(field.getName(), subObj);
      } else {
        doObject(subObj);
      }
    }
  }
  emitXMLFooter(cls);
}
```

I've omitted the code to actually emit the XML, but you get the picture. Look carefully at the lines in bold. You had to deal with primitives a little differently, but I'm lucky, because for this particular problem, I can treat all primitives the same. That's usually not the case. I'm really not done, because I also need to deal with arrays, leading to a whole new level of complexity.

Let's take another example. Here's an example that prints method names in Java:

```java
public static void printMethods(Object obj) throws Exception {
  Class cls = obj.getClass();
  Method[ ] methods = cls.getDeclaredMethods();
  for (int i=0; i < methods.length; i++) {
    Method method = methods[i];
    System.out.println("Method name:" + method.getName());
    Class parmTypes[ ] = method.getParameterTypes();
    for (int j = 0; j < parmTypes.length; j++) {
      System.out.print(" Parameter " + (j+1) + " type:");
      System.out.println(parmTypes[j]);
    }
  }
}
```

It's not as easy as simply grabbing the method names, because Java uses overloading, so you need to know the method name and parameter types to accurately identify a method. I'm going to give a Ruby example next, so if you want to compare apples to apples, just disregard the lines in bold.

Here's how easy reflection can be in Ruby. First, create an object. What class are we dealing with?

```
irb(main):001:0> i=4
=> 4
irb(main):002:0> i.class
=> Fixnum
```

Return a list of methods supported by a given object:

```
irb(main):003:0> i.methods
```

Print a neat list of the methods that Fixnum supports:

```
irb(main):003:0> i.methods.each {|m| puts m}
```

So, Ruby is very reflective. We've done the Java example (minus the lines in bold) in a single line of code. You can similarly find the instance variables, super classes, and so on. That's only the beginning of the power at your fingertips, though. You can also change classes, at runtime, on the fly. You can change a method on an object and leave the class untouched. Also, interceptors are child's play. You can use this metaprogramming to do some amazing things. The Ruby on Rails framework, featured in Chapter 7, shows an excellent example of what you can do.

I should point out that the primitives problem goes far beyond reflection. Look at the API for java.util.Array. You've got to treat arrays as their own kind of type. Java 1.5 makes matters worse by introducing generics. You run across similar problems whenever you need to deal with things generically, whether you're comparing, cloning, reflecting, or describing an object. It's a major problem that's encountered equally by people who use and build frameworks that deal with all types of user-defined objects. As we seek to find more ways to use objects transparently, the problem will only get worse.

Sound Foundations

I'm working on pure intuition here, but I do think that Java's successor will probably be object-oriented, and will be theoretically purer than Java. A purely object-oriented language makes things so much easier, especially when you start to consider metaprogramming, simplicity, learning curves, and increasing processing power. With Java's increasing emphasis on transparency, a cleaner approach will simplify many types of frameworks:

- Transparent persistence frameworks need only deal with objects and collections.
- XML binding frameworks would have a cleaner API, and a much cleaner implementation.
- Debugging frameworks like loggers could easily print values of any parameters.

Consistency is important, too. Languages with consistent naming and consistent behavior are far easier to learn. In general, the next language should be much more consistent, and cleaner. The characteristics in Table 5-4 would form a cleaner foundation for another 10 years of successful growth.

Table 5-4. Important language features that will help propel Java's successor

Rule	Description
Dynamic typing	Support dynamic typing for better productivity.
Rapid feedback loop	Minimize the time between making a change and seeing it execute.
User interface focus	Provide a productive, rich environment for building user interfaces.
Dynamic class model	Improve the ability to discover and change the parts of a class and runtime.
True OOP	Provide a conceptually pure implementation of OOP with no primitives and a single root for all objects.
Consistent and neat	The language should encourage code that's clean and maintainable.
Continuations	The language should enable important higher abstractions like continuations.

A Few Potential Suitors

Now that you've seen what the industry has to offer, let's take a quick review of some programming languages and identify some possible candidates. You'll see a more comprehensive treatment of the contenders in

Chapter 9. If you buy what I've been selling so far, you understand that for certain jobs, other languages may be better suited. I encourage you to try one of these languages every month or so.

If you've not been exposed to languages outside of C++, Basic, and Java, I've got to warn you that the experience can be unsettling. You'll be surprised at how much of your knowledge commutes, and how quickly you can grasp the essence that makes a given language so productive. You'll also be surprised at the fury that you can generate around the office just by peeking at alternatives—you may want to leave the nice car in the driveway and take the old Family Truckster to work for a while.

Perl

Perl is a scripting language, with a quirky syntax and a turbulent past. Here's a quick example that prints "Hi, Bruce":

```
my $name = "Bruce";
print "Hi, ", $x, "\n";
```

What I like

If raw productivity is your goal, perhaps Perl is a possible answer. It's dynamically typed, is highly productive, and has a small community established. It also has a fanatical following.

What I don't like

Perl does have a big downside. To this point, Perl's got a reputation of a write-only language: with its cryptic syntax, you can easily produce code that's very difficult to understand and maintain. Perl's OOP syntax, as with C++, is bolted on and awkward. As something more than a scripting language, Perl's reputation is probably a bit much to overcome.

Python

As dynamic programming languages go, Python has been one of the most successful. It's very close to Ruby in syntax and power, and it supports the language features that you'd want. Here's a brief snippet of Python code that counts to 10:

```
for x in xrange(10):
    print x
```

What I like

It has many of the features you need in an application's language: dynamic typing, a quick feedback loop, and a concise syntax. It's pretty fast, and it has a version that runs in the JVM (albeit slowly).

What I don't like

As much as I'd like it to be, I don't think Python is the ultimate answer. Ruby's inventor, Yukihiro Matsumoto (Matz), didn't use it because it's not object-oriented enough.* Python depends too much on whitespace, which most experts agree probably goes a bit too far. Others in the Python community aren't happy with the web development tools.† The web tools seem to be based on the Java stack, so there's no radical invention or departure. The community doesn't feel right. At times, it's too academic and too defensive.

The biggest hurdle for Python is its lack of compelling reasons to move away from Java. Python really needs a killer app. In the end, we've already formed our opinions. Python will be a moderately successful dynamic language, on the order of Smalltalk.

Ruby

Ruby is an object-oriented language created in the mid-1990s in Japan. The Ruby community grew steadily, and the language is now emerging beyond Japan. It's gained popularity in the United States only in the last couple of years.

What I like

Ruby has a beautiful syntax. It reads like English, and it miraculously stays out of your way. It's highly dynamic, and the educated core of the Ruby community works hard to produce clean, simple APIs. Ruby has strong web frameworks, and good support for XML and web services. Ruby has a couple of popular emerging frameworks, like Ruby on Rails. The web and XML frameworks are innovative and simple. The portable interpreter is fast, and it has the necessary plug-ins for the Apache web server. The standalone web interpreter, called Webrick, has several high-profile applications running on it. Most importantly, Ruby may have the killer app in Rails, which I'll discuss in detail in Chapter 7. This year will have four new Rails books and a strong

---

* Dave Thomas, *Programming Ruby* (Dallas: Pragmatic Bookshelf, 2005).
† *http://blog.ianbicking.org/why-web-programming-matters-most.html.*

publisher in the Pragmatic Bookshelf. Ruby doesn't have any political baggage that would turn away a potential commercial adopter. It's fairly mature.

What I don't like

In Japan, Ruby has good commercial financial backing and support. Outside of Japan, Ruby has an embarrassing lack of commercial backing. Its relatively small community shows in the dearth of niche frameworks. The JVM support is immature (although it is admittedly improving rapidly). Early attempts to produce a version of Ruby running on the JVM had a few false starts. Still, the JRuby framework has seen a resurgence of sorts in early 2005, so it may well produce a credible Java alternative on the JVM. Ruby is on the radar; it just needs a tighter affinity with the JVM and the continued success of Ruby on Rails.

PHP

PHP is a scripting language. With PHP, you effectively start with HTML, and mark it up with tags that can tie your application to a database, or other back-end systems. The tags get interpreted on the server, which returns pure HTML to the client. It's effectively a JSP. Here's a "Hello, World" app in PHP:

```
<html>
  <head>
    <title>Hello, world</title>
  </head>
  <body>
    <?php echo '<p>Hello world</p>'; ?>
  </body>
</html>
```

What I like

PHP success seems to be ramping up sharply, mostly on the strength of converted Visual Basic programmers. It's very well suited for its "sweet spot," controlling database access from a web page. It's easy to understand and easy to learn. PHP, more than any other language, is taking advantage of the frustration in the Visual Basic community due to changes in .NET.

What I don't like

PHP is theoretically awful. The model tightly couples the user interface and database together, and that's usually a bad idea, because changes in one can ripple through to the other. Since PHP grew rapidly and haphazardly with a heavy Perl influence, method names are often inconsistent, with some opting for underscores between words (`stream_get_line`) and some opting for concatenation (`readline`). PHP effectively has a reputation for productivity and rapid innovation at the expense of a consistent language that promotes sound architecture. As a Java programmer, you've probably already seen JSP pages that try to do too much. They're quick to write, but the solution bogs down in a hurry.

C# and Visual Basic

C# is effectively a Java clone. It has many of the same benefits and drawbacks. Visual Basic on the .NET environment seems to be losing momentum, because the older Visual Basic developers don't seem to have the same fervor for VB.NET. Microsoft has other languages as well. In the end, Microsoft will always have a core set of developers. That's effectively a closed ecosystem, though. It's limited by the success of the Windows platform, which is adopted broadly on the client, but decidedly less so on the server side. I'm not predicting success or failure; I just think that Microsoft languages depend on the success or failure of Microsoft platforms as a whole, rather than on the strengths or weaknesses of any given language in it.

Smalltalk

Invented in the early 1970s, Smalltalk is a well-established, hard-luck object-oriented language. Many see Smalltalk as the first object-oriented language, but it never really caught on commercially, despite some attempts as late as 1995 by IBM. It's hugely productive, slightly awkward, and quirky to the extreme. There is a vibrant, but small, Smalltalk community. Most of it is centered on a highly productive, continuation-based application development framework called Seaside, which we'll discuss in Chapter 8.

What I like

Smalltalk has a clean object model, incredible expressive power, and an intelligent design and community. It's got some solid free implementations, and a potential catalyst in Seaside. Glenn Vanderburg is fond of saying that all things will probably return to Smalltalk, but they won't be called Smalltalk anymore. When you see the influence of Smalltalk on languages like Ruby, that idea makes sense.

What I don't like

Smalltalk is not seen as a credible alternative. It just wasn't ever approachable enough. Smalltalk would have been a natural successor to C++ if Java hadn't come around first, but it was always too expensive, or too alien, or too obscure.

No Silver Bullet

You may have noticed that no language has all the characteristics we're seeking. That's not surprising. If one did, we'd be using it by now. Still, you can see that these languages do establish real strength in important areas. In the chapters to come, I'll take a deeper look at Ruby. Since it's not enough just to have a better language, we'll then investigate some potential killer apps.

CHAPTER 6

Ruby in the Rough

I stood on the bank of the Watauga River, looking at the 16-foot, Class V monster known as State Line Falls. It had five boulders in the current with four chutes running through them. Three of the slots were all but impassable, especially at this water level. The fourth was violent and intense. And yet, the approach was pretty easy, and I thought I could hit the line. Run this monster, or walk it. I had to choose.

Over the years, I've experienced a few moments like that one. Sometimes, I'd put my kayak on my shoulder and walk around. Other times, I decided that the line was good and my skills were up to the challenge, so I made the run. But this time, I simply stood, indecisive, with the wind and the spray from the falls washing over me.

I'm looking at a similar situation now. I do think that Java's leadership run, at least for applications, might be drawing to an end. But the stakes are unbelievably high should I decide to move. How can I know if the timing is right? Can I pick the right language? What do I risk?

I don't want this book to be an exhaustive review of programming languages. I'd like to point out one language and two frameworks (one in Ruby and one in Smalltalk) that have something special to offer. In this chapter, I introduce one possible alternative language, Ruby. I want to show you that some languages *can improve* on Java, but that doesn't mean that Ruby will succeed, or that it's the best possible alternative. The best that I can do, for now, is to show you *one possible alternative*, so you can see if the case makes sense.

About Ruby

Ruby is a dynamic, fully object-oriented language that's usually grouped with scripting languages. The scripting term, for languages like Ruby, Smalltalk, and Python, is a little too limited, so I'll use the term *applications language*. If you've used nothing but compiled languages like Java and C, get ready to have some fun. Ruby will turn you loose. I suggest that you install it (just go to *http://ruby-lang.org*), and type along. It comes with a primitive IDE, but the command line works well. Fire up a Ruby shell by typing **irb**. You'll get a shell prompt:

```
irb(main):001:0>
```

Ruby Is Fully OO

From here, you can evaluate Ruby statements. You'll frequently use irb to answer those tiny questions that come up often in programming. In Ruby, everything is an object, and if you type one alone, Ruby will return that object. Type **4** and press Enter:

```
irb(main):001:0> 4
=> 4
```

Unlike Java, numbers are objects, not primitives. For example, you can do this:

```
irb(main):008:0> 4.4765.round
=> 4
```

Even nil is a class, standing for nothing:

```
irb(main):009:0> nil.class
=> NilClass
```

You don't have to worry about primitives or wrappers at all. More importantly, you don't have to deal with those cases in an API. Ruby's reflection, persistence engines, and XML frameworks are all much simpler, because you don't have to deal with all the edge cases related to primitives and arrays of primitives.

Typing

Try to do an assignment without a declaration:

```
irb(main):011:0> n=1
=> 1
irb(main):012:0> n.class
=> Fixnum
```

So n has an object of type `Fixnum`. You didn't declare n at all. That's a strong hint that Ruby is dynamically typed. Now, assign something else to n:

```
irb(main):013:0> n="fish"
=> "fish"
irb(main):014:0> n.class
=> String
```

Now, n has a string. We changed the type of the variable i. More accurately, the type in Ruby is bound to the object, but not the thing that contains it. So Ruby *is* dynamically typed. Let's try to do something strange:

```
irb(main):015:0> n+4
TypeError: cannot convert Fixnum into String
        from (irb):15:in `+'
        from (irb):15
```

Ruby won't break its typing rules by coercing a string to a `Fixnum`. That means Ruby is strongly typed.* You can get its length by invoking the `size` method on n:

```
irb(main):016:0> n.size
=> 4
```

How do you know what methods a string supports? Just ask one:

```
irb(main):017:0> n.methods
=> ["send", "%", "rindex", "between?", "reject", "[ ]=", "split", "<<",
"object_id", "strip", "size", "singleton_methods", "downcase", "gsub!",
…and so on…
```

So, `String` supports a whole bunch of methods. Try to count them with the `size` method. If you've always used statically typed languages, you will probably underestimate the benefits. You've read that dynamic typing lets you focus on the right part of the problem at the right time. It eases your refactoring burden, and reduces the amount of code that you have to write and maintain.

Conditionals

Ruby's conditionals will remind you more of C than Java. In Ruby, `nil` and `false` evaluate to false, and everything else (including `true`) means true. Read that sentence again. Unlike C, 0 is true. You should also notice that `false` and `"false"` are different. One is the Boolean constant for false, and

---

* Actually, strongly typed is an oversimplification. Since you can change Ruby types indiscriminately, some might consider Ruby to have weaker typing. I'll stick with the oversimplified definition for this chapter.

one is a string. For example, puts "It's false." unless "false" returns nil, but puts "It's false." unless false will print It's false.

Ruby also has a few more conventions that you should know about. ? and ! are both valid in method names. By convention, methods ending in ? are tests. For example, nil? would test to see if a value is Nil. Methods ending in ! are potentially dangerous, because they have side effects. For example, a method called replace(in_string, sub_string, replacement) might return a string with the substring replaced, while replace!(in_string, sub_string, replacement) would modify the input string.

Like Java, Ruby has an if statement. Ruby also supports an unless statement that works the same way. You can use if or unless in block form, as you do in Java. You can also tack them onto the end of a line, to conditionally execute a single line of code. So, you can do something like this:

```
irb(main):099:0> def silence?(b)
irb(main):100:1>   puts    "SCREAM!" unless b
irb(main):101:1> end
=> nil
irb(main):106:0> silence? "False"
=> nil
irb(main):107:0> silence? "false"
=> nil
irb(main):108:0> silence? 0
=> nil
irb(main):109:0> silence? "quit kicking the cat"
=> nil
irb(main):110:0> silence? false
SCREAM!
=> nil
irb(main):111:0> silence? nil
SCREAM!
=> nil
```

Take a look at the silence? method. Ruby returns the value of the last statement, unless a method explicitly returns something. In this case, the statement puts "SCREAM!" unless b always returns nil. More importantly, the method prints SCREAM unless you pass it a true value.

Looping

Ruby has two conditional loops. You'll notice that many of Ruby's libraries help you by returning nil when they're done. If you're reading from standard input, you might do this:

```
irb(main):010:0> puts line while line=gets
one
```

```
one
two
two
^Z
=> nil
```

The loop continued until I entered the end-of-file character. Of course, you can also direct the input stream to a file. Plus you can use while at the beginning of a line, as long as you terminate it with an end:

```
irb(main):013:0> while line=gets
irb(main):014:1>    puts line
irb(main):015:1> end
```

You've already seen Until, the other looping construct. It works in exactly the same way, but it will fire the loop while the expression is false. You'll also see a for loop later, but that's just syntactic sugar.

Ranges

Java programmers typically will specify a range using an arithmetic expression, like this:

```
class Range {
  public static void main (String args[ ]) {
    int i = 4;
    if (2 < i && i < 8) System.out.println("true");
  }
}
```

You can do something similar in Ruby, but you've got another alternative. Ruby supports first-class range support. x..y represents values from x to y, inclusive. For example, 1..3 represents 1, 2, 3. You can include the 3 with a third period. As you can imagine, ranges in Ruby are objects:

```
irb(main):004:0> range=1..3
=> 1..3
irb(main):005:0> range.class
=> Range
```

You can also check to see if something is in a range, using the = = = operator:

```
irb(main):010:0> ('a'..'z') === 'h'
=> true
irb(main):011:0> ('a'..'z') === 'H'
=> false
irb(main):012:0> (1..10) === 5
=> true
```

You get more convenient syntactic sugar. Now, a for loop turns into this:

```
irb(main):021:0> for c in 'g'..'k'
irb(main):022:1>    puts c
```

```
irb(main):023:1> end
g
h
i
j
k
```

for/in loops also work with Arrays and Hashes. Ranges introduce ===, another type of comparison. Next, you'll see a third type of comparison, called match, which you'll use with regular expressions.

Regular Expressions

Java has an API that supports regular expressions. Ruby builds regular expressions into the syntax. Some like regular expressions and others do not. To me, they're a critical part of dealing with strings. Just like any other type of programming, you can take them too far. If you've got 16 consecutive backslashes, it's probably time to refactor. Still, they can be much more useful than similar code, handwritten to recognize certain patterns.

In Ruby, you'll define a regular expression between slashes. You'll match regular expressions like this:

```
irb(main):027:0> regex = /better/
=> /better/
irb(main):028:0> regex.class
=> Regexp
irb(main):029:0> "Mine is bigger" =~ regex
=> nil
irb(main):030:0> "Mine is better" =~ regex
=> 8
```

Ruby returns the index of the character at the match. Ruby regular expressions are much more powerful than I can show you here. I'll just say that Java developers spend at least half of their time dealing with strings. When you think about it, servlets, XML strings, configuration files, deployment descriptors, and application data can all be strings. To parse them effectively, you need first-class pattern matching, such as regular expressions and ranges. Java 1.5 closes the gap some, but not completely.

Containers

Ruby containers are like Java's collections. You just saw an array. Like Java, arrays are objects: [1,2,3].class returns Array. Unlike Java, everything in an array is also an object. Ruby also has a Hash. Like Java's HashMaps, a Ruby Hash is an object. Unlike Java's HashMap, a Ruby Hash also has some syntactic sugar. You use braces instead of brackets, and you use **key=>value** to define one key-value pair, like this:

```
irb(main):011:0> numbers={0=>"zero", 1=>"one", 2=>"two", 3=>"three"}
=> {0=>"zero", 1=>"one", 2=>"two", 3=>"three"}
irb(main):012:0> 4.times {|i| puts numbers[i]}
zero
one
two
three
```

Like Java collections, Ruby containers hold objects, and they need not be homogeneous. In version 1.5, Java's generics let you build type-safe collections. You could modify Ruby's `Array` or `Hash` to make them type safe. (Remember, you can modify any of Ruby's classes directly. It's a dynamic language.) While Ruby doesn't have dozens of types of containers like Java does, you will notice some benefits immediately:

- Since there's no distinction between primitives and other objects, you can put literally anything into any given container, and you can nest them easily.
- Since everything inherits from `object`, everything has a hash code.
- The language gives you the same syntactic sugar for hashes as for arrays.
- Code blocks make iteration tighter and easier.

If you're a big Java collections user who's used a dynamic language before, you probably noticed that Java collections often feel wrong. You have to circumvent static type checking, because you're adding something to a collection as an object, and you're forced to cast it to something else when you retrieve it. Iteration is painful and awkward. A collection doesn't feel like a standard array, which can possibly contain primitives.

Ruby containers will feel altogether different. You won't have to deal with the maddening type casts or generic syntax. Code blocks simplify iteration. You don't see too many types of collections, but don't let that fool you. Using the rich methods, you can use `Array` as a list, queue, stack, or any other type of ordered collection. For instance, let's use `Array` as a stack:

```
irb(main):001:0> stack=[1,2,3]
=> [1, 2, 3]
irb(main):002:0> stack.push "cat"
=> [1, 2, 3, "cat"]
irb(main):003:0> stack.pop
=> "cat"
irb(main):004:0> stack
=> [1, 2, 3]
```

Similarly, you can use Hash whenever you need a set, dictionary, or any type of unordered collection. You'll find yourself doing more with collections, and less customized iteration.

Files

Iterating through a file works much like iterating through a collection. You'll create a new file and pass it a code block. For example, here's a simple GREP:

```
File.open(ARGV[0]) do |file|
  rx = Regexp.new(ARGV[1])
  while line=file.gets
    puts line if line =~ rx
  end
end
```

To use it, type it into a file called *grep.rb*. Then, you can call it (outside of irb) like this:

```
ruby grep.rb filename regex
```

Notice what you don't see. You don't have to close the file or manage exceptions. This implementation makes sure the file will be closed if an exception occurs. You're effectively using a library that specifies everything on the outside of a control loop that iterates through a file. Ruby does the repetitive dirty work for you, and you customize the inside of the control loop with a code block.

Why Should You Care?

By now, you should be getting a feel for the power and simplicity of Ruby. You can probably see how the lines of code go down and the abstraction goes up. You might think it doesn't make any difference. You could lean ever harder on your development environments and on code generation tools like XDoclet, and shield yourself from some of the problem, but let me tell you: *lines of code matter!*

- *You still have to understand anything that your tools generate.* I work with dozens of people every year that don't understand the SQL that Hibernate cranks out, and others who have to maintain generated code, after they tailor it for their needs.

- *The more code you have, the more bugs it can hide.* Unit testing can take you only so far. You'll still need to inspect code to enhance it or maintain it.

- *Writing code is not the only cost.* You also need to consider the cost of training, maintaining, and extending your code.

- *Each code generation technique that you use limits your flexibility.* Most Java developers now depend on tools to do more and more. Each tool that you adopt carries a cost. I'm an IDEA man, but some of my customers use Eclipse. I'm nowhere nearly as effective on it, so my customer loses something when I am forced to use it. XDoclet increases the feedback cycle.

- *Java developers rely increasingly on XML for configuration.* Remember, configuration is still code. Developers from other languages often find Java's over-reliance on XML configuration annoying. We use so much configuration outside of the language because configuration in Java is painful and tedious. We do configuration in XML rather than properties because...well, because overuse of XML in Java is a fad. Meanwhile, configuration in Ruby is usually clean and comfortable.

You may be willing to pay the costs related to lines of code, but you should also consider higher abstractions. With Java, you must use unsightly iterators. With Ruby, you wind up building the iteration strategies into your containers and reusing that logic.

Said another way, Java customization usually happens with an outside-in strategy. You build big chunks of reusable code that fill out the inside of your applications. But that's only one kind of customization. For many jobs, you'd like to keep a generic implementation of a job, and customize a few lines of code on the *inside* of a method. Iterating through a JDBC loop, processing a file, and iterating through a collection are only a few examples of this strategy. Some Java developers call this strategy *inversion of control*.

Ruby lets you program with both styles, as shown in Figure 6-1. Code written with that strategy is a joy to maintain, and it hides repetition from you. To be fair, some Java frameworks, like Spring, do some of this for you as well, but it's not as easy in Java, and this style of programming is not nearly as common, since you have to use the heavyweight anonymous inner class to do so. In dynamic languages like Ruby and Smalltalk, this programming strategy gives you tremendous intellectual freedom, both in the frameworks that you use and in the frameworks that you build.

Applying Some Structure

Both Ruby and Java are object-oriented languages. Both support object models with single inheritance. Still, you're going to see some differences between Ruby and Java:

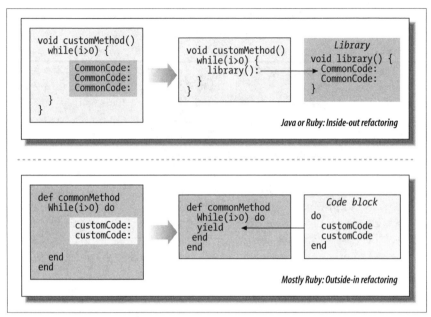

Figure 6-1. Java programmers refactor the inside of a loop; code blocks let Ruby developers refactor the outside of a loop, too

- In Java, the smallest application is a class. In Ruby, everything is an object, so you can evaluate primitives, expressions, code blocks, and scripts. They all are objects, and all are valid Ruby.

- In Java, class definitions are static. In Ruby, you can modify your classes on the fly. When you see a class definition, if the class already exists, the new definition will modify the class that's already there.

- Ruby supports mixins and Java does not. Think of a mixin as an interface, plus an implementation, that you can attach to a class.

- In Ruby, everything returns some value, and that value is typed dynamically, so you won't see a return in the method definition.

- In Ruby, method parameters and instance variables are not typed; but the instances themselves are typed.

For the most part, you can still use your OO design skills in Ruby as you did in Java. You'll also see some common design patterns, like model-view-controller.

David Heinemeier Hansson: Ruby
Creator of Ruby on Rails

David Heinemeier Hansson is the programmer of Basecamp, Backpack, and Ta-da List under the commercial banner of 37signals, but he's also an avid open source contributor through the Rails web development framework and Instiki—one of the most popular Ruby applications. He's intensely focused on doing something about the sorry state of programmer productivity, be it through software, like Rails, or through practices, like Less Software.

Why is Rails so much more productive than similar Java stacks?

DHH: Ruby allows Rails to implement *convention* over *configuration* at runtime, which not only removes needless repetition but also relieves the programming cycle from being bogged down by compilation, code generation, and deployment. It brings the immediacy of change-and-reload from languages like PHP together with modern software techniques like domain-driven, test-driven development, and patterns. It's quick without being dirty; it's scalable without being heavy.

What are the three most important features in Ruby that you use in Rails?

DHH: First, metaprogramming. You can manipulate a class while it's being defined. You can create domain-specific languages, because you've got hooks everywhere into the life cycle of classes and objects. It's a framework builder's dream.

Second, open classes. Active Record consists of around 10 layers that are all applied to the base class. It keeps the API simple. You don't use 10 different classes, and Rails still satisfies the requirement of a maintainable code base. It's also been helpful to be able to extend the base classes and fix bugs in the standard library between releases.

Third, everything is an object, with exceptions. You can work procedurally on top of the object orientation, but that's the order of business. It makes for an incredibly consistent experience that really makes "The Principle of Least Surprise" come true. You can guess the names and behavior of Ruby classes more often than not.

What makes Java limiting to you?	**DHH:** On an "every language can do anything" level, there's nothing that inherently limits what Java can do, but there's certainly different comfort zones for different languages and people. I can't stand repeating myself. I can't stand a long feedback cycle. I can't stand computing in my head or writing by hand what the compiler should be able to figure out from my intentions.
	Java doesn't make me a happy programmer; Ruby fills me with joy. I don't want to work with tools that don't make me happy. So, if that were the only choice, I would pick a different career where I could work with tools that made me happy.
Are Ruby and Rails ready for production web applications?	**DHH:** Not only ready, but already running. Basecamp, the application that birthed Rails, has been running for more than a year and is widely successful. Upstarts working on the Web 2.0 frontier are picking Ruby on Rails in droves. 43things.com and Odeo.com are just two examples of that.

Classes

Ruby is object-oriented. I've shown you how to use Ruby objects, but not yet how to create one. Let's make a class called `Calculator`. Create a file called *calculator.rb* that looks like this:

```
class Calculator

  def initialize
    @total=0
  end

  def add(x)
    @total += x
  end

  def subtract(x)
    @total -= x
  end

end
```

You've declared three methods. Ruby will call `initialize` when it creates a new object, such as this calculator. Notice that `initialize` defines an instance variable called `@total`. In Ruby, instance variables start with @, class variables start with @@, and global variable start with $. Now, in `irb`, you can load the file and use the calculator.

```
irb(main):005:0> require 'Calculator'
=> true
irb(main):006:0> c=Calculator.new
=> #<Calculator:0x28b4a98 @total=0>
irb(main):007:0> c.add 100

=> 100
irb(main):008:0> c.subtract 40
=> 60
```

And it works, just like you'd expect. Ruby developers take advantage of *open classes*. I'm going to change the definition of Calculator, but keep in mind that we still have c, an instance of Calculator. I actually open up the definition of the class again like this:

```
irb(main):009:0> class Calculator
irb(main):010:1>   def reset
irb(main):011:2>     @total = 0
irb(main):012:2>   end
irb(main):013:1> end
```

I just added a method called reset. I also could have changed an existing method.

```
irb(main):014:0> c.reset
=> 0
```

That's amazing. I changed the class definition of an existing class. That's a useful capability for debugging, iterative programming, and metaprogramming. Ruby also lets you subclass. To subclass, you use the < operator:

```
irb(main):015:0> class IrsCalculator < Calculator
irb(main):016:1>   def add(x)
irb(main):017:2>     x = x / 2 if x>0
irb(main):018:2>     super
irb(main):019:2>   end
irb(main):020:1> end
=> nil
```

You can use it, and IrsCalculator will take a little off the top for you:

```
irb(main):027:0> c=IrsCalculator.new
=> #<IrsCalculator:0x28b6b80 @total=0>
irb(main):028:0> c.add 100
=> 50
```

These concepts should look familiar to you. Classes package instance data and methods together. An instance of a class is an object. All classes have single parents, and eventually inherit from Object, with the exception of Object:

```
irb(main):031:0> Class.superclass
=> Module
irb(main):032:0> Module.superclass
```

```
=> Object
irb(main):033:0> Object.superclass
=> nil
```

Using Mixins

To implement a mixin, Ruby uses a concept called a *module*. A module lets you group together methods and classes. You can't instantiate a module, and a module doesn't stand alone. A module isn't a class, but it does have its own namespace. Modules form the foundation of classes and mixins.

Mixins are not new. Smalltalk supported them back in 1971. Recall that a mixin is an interface with an implementation. That means you can group together a set of methods that many classes may need to use.

Look at this contrived little example. To build the friendliest possible application, you may want to build a mixin to greet any object by name. You'd code it like this:

```
irb(main):021:0> module Greetable
irb(main):022:1>   def greet
irb(main):023:2>     puts "Hello, " + self.name
irb(main):024:2>   end
irb(main):025:1> end
=> nil
```

Then, you can include this code in a class called Person:

```
irb(main):011:0> class Person
irb(main):012:1>   include Greetable
irb(main):013:1>   def initialize(name, age)
irb(main):014:2>     @name=name
irb(main):015:2>     @age=age
irb(main):016:2>   end
irb(main):017:1>   attr_reader :name
irb(main):018:1> end
=> nil
```

You can use this code in Person:

```
irb(main):039:0> person=Person.new("Bruce",40)
=> #<Person:0x2a970a0 @age=40, @name="Bruce">
irb(main):040:0> person.greet
Hello, Bruce
=> nil
```

While mixins seem interesting, this code probably smells wrong to you. Unless you could better integrate the Person methods in the mixin, it's just a recipe to make bad design decisions: you can include stuff that doesn't really have anything to do with Person into Person. But it's more powerful than that. You can separate an aspect, or a capability, into a mixin. What makes mixins so powerful is this: you can also access Person's class methods in your module. In fact, we used Person.name, in the module, before we had even defined Person. If it sounds confusing, just look at the following module. inspect is a class method that puts the contents of an object in string form:

```
irb(main):147:0> module Reversible
irb(main):148:1>   def inspect
irb(main):149:2>     super.reverse
irb(main):150:2>   end
irb(main):151:1> end
=> nil
```

Note that you haven't defined a class yet, but you're still using the inspect class method. That may seem strange until you include the module in the Calculator class that we made before:

```
irb(main):152:0> class Person
irb(main):153:1>   include Reversible
irb(main):154:1> end
=> Person
```

Now you've included the module, and it has a class. It's now a mixin. You can call any new instance methods that it defines. It will assume the class that you add it to. Look at what happens when you instantiate it:

```
irb(main):155:0> p=Person.new("Bruce", 40)
=> >"ecurB"=eman@ ,04=ega@ 0711c82x0:nosreP<#
```

irb actually calls inspect when you instantiate an object. Did you see the garbled line at the bottom? It's actually "Person:0x28c1170 @age=40, @name=\ "Bruce\"" in reverse. That's impressive. Now, you can add a mixin that can inspect the class, and integrate the most intimate details of the class into the mixin. And you can do all of this integration before a class even exists. I can use mixins for things like security or persistence. Java developers often resort to AOP to get the capability of mixins.

Interceptors

I've said that Java framework developers these days place an ever-increasing value on techniques that change the behavior of an existing class, without changing its code. One such technique is *method interception*. JBoss and Spring use method interception to attach arbitrary services to a POJO. With Ruby, interception is easy. You simply take a method, rename it, and put another method in its place (see Figure 6-2).

For example, let's say that my friend, Dave Thomas, asks me to watch his laptop for a few minutes before his big Ruby presentation. I could go to his Ruby shell and enter this little gem based on an example from his book,

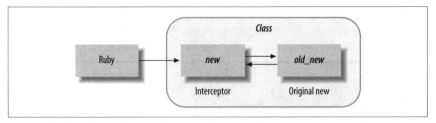

Figure 6-2. In Ruby, to do method interception, you simply rename and replace a method, with the new implementation calling the old

Programming Ruby (Pragmatic Bookshelf). This version intercepts new, as you can see in Figure 6-2. I simply rename the original and call it from the replacement new. The interceptor will print out a message whenever Ruby creates a new object. Here's how easy it is:

```
class Class
  alias_method :original_new, :new
  def new(*args)
    result = original_new(*args)
    print "Unattended laptop error. "
    return result
  end
end
```

And when Dave gets back to teach his class, he'll get a nice surprise when he does anything that creates an object (which is pretty much anything in Ruby):

```
irb(main):009:0> i=[1,2,3]
Unattended laptop error. Unattended laptop error. Unattended laptop error.
Unattended laptop error. Unattended laptop error. Unattended laptop error.
Unattended laptop error. Unattended laptop error. Unattended laptop error.
Unattended laptop error. Irb(main):010:0>
```

That's an interceptor in eight lines of code. You get extra credit if you know which 10 objects get created. You don't have any Java proxies, code generation, or aspect-oriented programming. Of course, you'll not want to try this with the real Dave. That would be like throwing a firecracker under Albert Einstein's car. Like Albert and the atom, you don't want to unleash this kind of power without knowing where all the energy is going to go.

AOP

Java developers depend on AOP with increasing frequency. AOP lets you add services to your POJO without modifying any code. AOP helps you control the flow of your application, such as adding custom methods at interesting points—for instance, before or after a method executes. In particular, you'll often see AOP for:

Debugging or logging

AOP lets you add debugging or logging code everywhere that you need it, with very little syntax.

Declarative services

EJB used a container to provide services. You would specify the service with configuration rather than code. Lightweight containers do the same thing with AOP. You'll often see interceptors manage transactions, security, and remoting.

Mixins

Java doesn't provide mixins, but you can simulate them with AOP.

David Heinemeier Hansson and Jim Weirich, Two Ruby Experts: AOP in Ruby

Jim Weirich is a software consultant for Compuware. He has worked with real-time data systems for testing jet engines, networking software for information systems, and image processing software for the financial industry. Jim is active in the Ruby community, contributing to several Ruby projects including Rake and RubyGems.

Why hasn't AOP taken off for Ruby?

DHH: A standardized AOP framework has never really taken off in Ruby because the language itself already supports most of the desirable functionality of AOP.

The following is an example from Action Pack, the controller/view part of Rails. And here follows the code block that injects the layout functionality into the original render method:

```
base.class_eval do
  alias_method :render_without_layout, :render
  alias_method :render, :render_with_layout
end
```

So, we rename the original render method to render_without_layout, which we can then call from the enhanced render_with_layout method. And finally, we make the improved render_with_layout method take the place of render. So, we're hot-swapping out behavior of a base class with improved functionality without changing the public interface and without cluttering the base class with the enhancements directly. The next version of Ruby will take this a step further by including AOP-like constructs right in the language with pre, post, and wrap conditions.

JW: The metaprogramming capabilities of Ruby lie so close to the surface and are quite accessible to the average Ruby programmer. I suspect that most of the problems addressed by AOP are addressed by metaprogramming in Ruby.

Here's one example from the standard library. Date objects are immutable, so once you calculate the day of the week for any given date object, you could store that result and return it in later invocations without redoing the entire calculation. The code to check for a previously calculated value is simple enough to write, but it is tedious to implement it in each of the 13 or so methods in Date that could take advantage of it.

The author of the Date class took this approach. He wrote each method as if it would recalculate the value every time it was called (i.e., no special checking for previous values). Then he wrote a class method called once that takes a list of method names. The once method did the following: created an alias for the named method; made that alias private; and created a new method with the original name that checked for a previously calculated value before calling the original code (via the alias). In other words, the once method rewrote existing methods to calculate its return value once and store the result.

Looking for further evidence that AOP-like solutions are easy in Ruby metaprogramming? The AspectR library adds some simple AOP operations to Ruby. Although not as complete as its sister library, AspectJ, from the Java world, the library itself is orders of magnitude smaller...clocking in at around 210 lines of code.

I'm not an AOP expert by any stretch of the imagination. But I've seen the relatively narrow set of problems addressed by AOP, and the wide range of metaprogramming solutions that keep cropping up in the Ruby world. Perhaps it is not Ruby that needs AOP, but Java that needs metaprogramming!

Of course, AOP is a much broader tool, and if it is successful, the typical use cases obviously will grow in scope and power. Right now, though, Java developers most frequently use the power of AOP through frameworks like Spring.

You can look at interceptors as a more primitive tool to accomplish the same sorts of things. The JBoss framework and containers like HiveMind use interceptors to provide a wide range of services, like transactions. For Ruby developers, AOP is not quite as urgent, because you've already got robust tools to deal with these kinds of concerns:

- You can use interceptors. These let you add services to any object at any time. It's as easy as renaming one method and introducing another.

- You can use mixins, even attaching them at runtime. You could easily make all of the methods on a domain model secure, for example.

- You can use hooks. Ruby provides hooks so that you can inject custom code at certain well-defined locations. The next version of Ruby will support hooks called __before, __after, and __wrap.

In short, Ruby can already solve many AOP-like problems without AOP, and will add AOP-like features in the very near future. Some Ruby programmers are concerned that AOP code may be more difficult to maintain. The core value of AOP that's not yet supported in Ruby is the ability to specify a point cut quickly and efficiently, which lets you use regular expressions to define interceptors wherever you need them. Ruby already has the core features that should make point cuts easy to implement:

- You can quickly query for the methods that an object supports.

- You can match regular expressions.

- You can invoke a method with a string.

- You'll soon (Ruby 2.0) be able to hook Ruby methods with before, after, and wrap.

- Ruby is very friendly to configure. You can specify the point cuts in Ruby, without requiring XML or a whole new syntax, like AspectJ.

Given these capabilities, AOP becomes a very lightweight feature. Right now, Ruby developers prefer to implement AOP-like features, piecemeal, in a style that best fits the architecture.

Dependency Injection

The difference dependency injection in Java and Ruby is a little tougher to understand for Java developers. In Java, dependency injection is rapidly changing the way that we build applications. It's a relatively simple concept:

```
class Speaker {
  void speak(String words) {
    System.out.println(words);
  }
}
class Consumer {
  Speaker mySpeaker;
  void saySomething() {
    mySpeaker.speak("something");
  }
}
```

Notice Consumer. It doesn't instantiate Speaker. That job goes to a third party. We'll call it Container:

```
class Container {
  public static void main(String[ ] args) {
    Speaker speaker=new Speaker( );
    Consumer consumer=new Consumer( );
    consumer.mySpeaker = speaker;
    consumer.saySomething( );
  }
}
```

You can make some simple improvements. You can encapsulate mySpeaker with a getter and setter. You can then extract an interface called Speaker, and provide implementations for FrenchSpeaker, EnglishSpeaker, and SpanishSpeaker. You can also make a configuration file, in Java or XML, describing all the objects that you want to treat this way.

You'd then have most of what you'd need for a basic dependency injection container: configuration, third-party life cycle control, and the ability to loosen the coupling between Speaker and Consumer. With a dependency injection container, you could change implementations of Speaker without changing any code in any of the consumers. You could also inject a test implementation of Speaker without impacting the base code, a critical technique in Java for test-first development. You'd also have a consistent strategy for configuration.

A few things come up right off the bat when you look at dependency injection in Ruby. First, Java's not very good at configuration, but Ruby lets you represent structured data quite well, often with far less invasive syntax than XML. You also can solve many of the coupling problems by changing the definition of a class on the fly. It's easier, for example, to inject those mock objects into hard-to-reach places.

Some developers in Ruby seem to think dependency injection is important and that the idea will have a place in the Ruby mainstream, given time. It should come as no surprise to you that Ruby has an outstanding dependency injection framework called Needles.

Others tend to think that dependency injection should happen in spots, instead of with a single, general-purpose framework. Since it's easy to change a class definition on the fly, you can easily inject the behavior that you need without adding another layer of complexity, across the application. Most of the Ruby programming community seems to be converging on the idea that Ruby's overall dynamic design makes dependency injection unnecessary for all but the most complex applications (see the sidebar, "Jim Weirich, Jamis Buck, and David Heinemeier Hansson, Three Ruby Experts: Does Ruby Need Dependency Injection?").

Jim Weirich, Jamis Buck, and David Heinemeier Hansson, Three Ruby Experts: Does Ruby Need Dependency Injection?

Jamis Buck has been writing Ruby code since late 2001, and has written (among various other things) two Ruby dependency injection containers, Ruby bindings for SQLite and SQLite3, and an SSH client library for Ruby. During the day (and some evenings), he works for 37signals, programming in Ruby and Rails. Jamis lives in Provo, Utah, with his wife and two children.

Does Ruby need dependency injection?

JW: The question should not be if Ruby needs dependency injection, but whether a particular application or framework needs dependency injection. DI is a tool to help you build decoupled programs, but it comes with some conceptual baggage. You start using DI when the pain of coupling outweighs the cost of the additional complexity. In some languages, this pain comes fairly quickly. But in Ruby, the pain is mitigated by the natural tendency for looser coupling in a dynamically typed language, so the benefits of dependency injection occur much later in the cost curve. In addition, there are some very simple techniques to lower the cost of coupling without using a formal dependency injection framework.

And finally, when your application/framework does grow to the point that dependency injection becomes interesting, you will find that a simple (i.e., less than 30 lines of code) dependency injection library will fill most of your needs.

JB: I wrote two very different DI containers for Ruby, about a year or two ago. I pushed them both pretty hard, and I worked hard to educate the Ruby community about DI, but the fact is that I really came to understand this: the dynamic nature of Ruby really does obviate the need for most of what DI does in Java land.

DHH: We actually looked into basing the configuration of services in Rails off Needle, but all the problems I was trying to solve with DI could be solved much more simply. For example, dependency injection makes it easier to inject mocks into hard-to-get places. Consider a payment class that initializes a payment gateway to authorize and charge a credit card. Without DI, it might look like this:

```
class Payment < ActiveRecord::Base
  belongs_to :credit_card
  def capture
    PaymentGateway.capture(amount, credit_card)
  end
end
```

Now in a language like Java, the direct use of PaymentGateway would be a rather nasty dependency on a concrete class that would make it hard to mock and hence test. Not so in Ruby. And especially not in Rails, since it has specific support for mocks of this type. We can stub out exactly the methods that need to be stubbed out, but nothing else. So, for the payment gateway, we'd just do this:

```
require "original/payment_gateway"

class PaymentGateway
  cattr_accessor :desired_result

  def self.capture(amount, credit_card)
    Response.new(desired_result)
  end
end
```

We're now able to specify PaymentGateway.desired_result = : success and the partially mocked out PaymentGateway will comply, using all the rest of the real infrastructure; just not calling the actual remote system over the wire.

Breaking It Down

That's a 30-minute tour through Ruby. I'm not saying that Ruby is the next great language, but rather, that Ruby makes some of the hard things in Java easy. More and more of the top independent consultants are looking for ways to make more money working in Ruby, or other languages that are more dynamic. The Java community is spending an amazing amount of money and brainpower on making Java more dynamic. Dependency injection and aspect-oriented programming are groundbreaking ideas for Java, and they are only now getting serious commercial traction. For Java developers, these ideas represent better transparency and simpler application development.

Collapsing Under the Weight of Abstraction?

My playtime in Ruby makes another, more powerful idea, clearer. As we stretch Java in increasingly unnatural directions, there's a cost. AOP and dependency injection are near-trivial exercises in Ruby, but they force Java developers to learn new programming models, deal with XML, and introduce increasingly complex syntax. With each new metaprogramming concept that we bake into Java, it's looking more and more like all of that complexity is trying to drive us somewhere. The net effect is to push Java further and further into the enterprise niche, and make it less and less accessible to the average Joe. Contrast that situation with Ruby, where dependency injection and AOP don't consume your focus; you're free to apply those ideas in spots right where you need them.

I do think that Ruby, with Rails, is a near-ideal solution for that sweet spot that we've pushed: a web-based frontend for a relational database. I've already said that I'm using Ruby in a commercial application. My customer demanded productivity and a price point that I couldn't achieve in any other way. I also still recommend Java to many of my clients. They need complex frameworks that Ruby does not yet support, or they depend on a core set of developers that have already been trained, or they have so much legacy code in Java that change would be impractical.

In the next chapter, I'll make these arguments real. I'll show you how to build a web-based application, from scratch, to access a relational database with a web application. Then, I'll show you what another killer app might be, for another language.

CHAPTER 7

Ruby on Rails

As I screamed uphill toward the 3-foot ledge, the voice inside my head said "Don't fight it. Go for it." Knowledgeable mountain bikers called the move *the lunge*, but I had neither named nor internalized it yet. My brain rebelled against the completely unintuitive idea that a moving biker could thrust his bike forward near the top of such a ledge and accomplish anything other than a spectacular crash, but I'd seen it work. I hit the ledge with speed and thrust the bike forward by simply pushing on the handlebars, and the bike was over the ledge. On some level, I didn't understand that success was a possibility. Though I was safely on top, I stepped off my pedals anyway—I'd been sure that I would fail. The idea seemed too much like flying by pulling hard enough on your shoestrings. Learning this mysterious lunge would take a while.

Like the lunge, metaprogramming also seems a little unnatural to me. Then again, I've been coding in Java and C for most of my professional career. If you want to experience the power of a framework that uses metaprogramming extensively, Rails is the gold standard.

The Numbers Game

As a fairly content Java programmer, I really didn't go searching for an alternative. In some ways, Rails found me. Dave Thomas and I speak at the same conference. I taught several sessions on the Spring framework with Hibernate, and I was very happy with my productivity. Of course, compared with EJB, I was very productive. Dave pointed out that even in Hibernate with Spring, you tend to repeat yourself on a fairly regular basis.

I reflected on David's comments. To make a persistent domain model, you need to specify a database table with its fields and indexes, specify an object domain model with a class (repeating yourself) and a field as an attribute (repeating yourself), and add accessors for that field (repeating again and again). Then, you need to build a mapping with the database table (repeating again) and the class name (and yet again). Finally, your mapping must specify each database column and the corresponding database field (repeating each column twice more). Of course, most sane Java developers do not do all of that repeating. They let the tools do most of it for them, but now your programming model dictates your tool set, your development experience, and generates more lines of code to maintain. I came to the conclusion that ORM makes sense when the domain model and object model are sufficiently different, and I decided I'd take the slight productivity hit and be compensated with better performance and the possibilities of better mapping.

A Blinding Flash of Insight

As I've said, I worked with a company that builds safety software for a manufacturing plant. We effectively build a web user interface to manage a complex domain model. We decided to build this application with a lightweight Java stack of Spring, Hibernate, and Web Work. We moved pretty quickly, and were pleased with our progress. We were proud of our accomplishments, because we'd rewritten a one-year Microsoft application in four months with Java. Naturally, as we accumulated a bigger code base, coding began to take longer.

Over time, Dave's arguments nagged at my subconscious. Dave and my business partner had the same conversations. As luck would have it, over the same week, we tried building a part of the application in Rails. I banged out the model and scaffolding in a couple of days. With his stronger HTML experience, Justin got further than I did. He actually implemented the whole application in Rails in four nights. The Rails version shocked us in another way—it was actually faster!

Justin Gehtland: A Ruby on Rails Case Study

Coauthor of *Better, Faster, Lighter Java*

Justin Gehtland is the co-founder of Relevance, a consulting/training organization based in Durham, North Carolina. He's the coauthor of the Jolt-winning book, Better, Faster, Lighter Java, *and has been developing applications of all sizes since the early 1990s. Over the last six years, he has delivered products using Java, .NET, LAMP, and now, Ruby on Rails.*

You've recently moved a Java project to Ruby on Rails. What Java frameworks did the application use?

JG: The original stack was the usual suspects in the lightweight movement: Spring and Hibernate, plus a little JSTL on the frontend (so that the end customers could more easily customize the interface). I was using the ACEGI security framework for authentication and authorization, but only to authenticate against a local database of accounts.

What surprised you the most about the experience?

JG: After porting the app and talking about the experience, I was really surprised by the heated discussion it generated. There's that old saw about disruptive technologies; if the temperature gauge on the discussion is any indication, Rails is clearly in the disruptive category.

From a technology perspective, I was surprised at the level of performance I was able to achieve. The Rails version of the app was fast, and faster even than the original Java version. That's partially due to a better understanding of the domain (rewrites always take lessons learned into account), partially due to a lack of performance tuning on the original stack, but mostly due to the fact that the performance gains with Rails are easy to achieve. The page and action caching strategies are right at the surface, and it's easy to manage their life cycle. I was able to max out the web server's ability to serve pages. I literally couldn't get it to go any faster.

Is Rails ready to usurp Java?

JG: Ruby isn't going to outstrip Java on a straight road. The JVM is tuned, and tuned, and tuned again to optimize byte code execution. But Ruby on Rails shines on the turns. Its integrated stack, dynamic language, and lack of a write/compile/test/deploy cycle means it handles better. For this application, it was like racing a Miata against a funny car on a mountain road. The funny car has more horsepower, but it just ends up driving straight all the time.

What are the top three things that made Ruby so much more productive?

JG: I'd have to say that the dedication to smart defaults is the primary benefit to Ruby on Rails. Ben Galbraith has said it several times, and I concur. Since Rails always lets you override any of its defaults, you are never in danger of getting stuck in a corner, but for the most part, you can create an application and ignore 90% of what would be surfaced in configuration files in another framework.

Second, I really was surprised at how much of a difference the lack of the configure/compile/deploy/test cycle really makes. Saving a change and launching the tests while reloading the browser just seemed so instantaneous comparatively. I don't know that it made me more productive, but it made me *feel* more productive.

Lastly, the dynamic nature of Ruby really shined for me. I did need some common pieces of functionality in the app that really belonged back at the framework level. Instead of having to delve into the source to add them, I just extended the classes I needed to at runtime. That kind of extensibility is anathema (and usually impossible) in a more statically typed language.

Making the Commitment

Of course, playing with a prototype and getting a customer to switch from tried and proven Java to a relatively unknown framework on an unknown language was an altogether different proposition. I had a conversation with the start-up's owner, and the results surprised me. He jumped at the chance to move. I guess I shouldn't be surprised. We simply couldn't ignore the differences in raw productivity between the frameworks.

In a start-up environment, productivity rules all other concerns. Since you don't often have the resources of your competition, you need to iterate *fast*. You can get some leverage by working longer hours and cutting bureaucracy. If you can generate an edge with technology, you've got to take that opportunity. In an increasingly competitive global landscape, we'll all need to act more like start-ups. If a framework makes you a mere 120% faster, you might be tempted to stay with a safer language like Java. But if you can be 400% faster or more, I don't think you can ignore the difference.

Remember, my premise is that Java is drifting away from its base. Most of us need to build web applications on relational databases. Language issues are important, but Java's drivers are so focused on hard-core enterprise problems that they're not making any progress on this simple core problem. If Rails doesn't step into this gap, something else will.

Some Numbers

I'm going to give you some performance and productivity numbers based on experience. I recognize the numbers are imperfect, for a whole lot of reasons. In some ways, the deck was stacked against Rails:

- The Ruby application implemented more customer requirements. By the time Justin realized that his experience was important, he'd implemented some features that never made it into the Java version.

- Justin was a recognized expert in Java, but had never used Ruby in a project, and had never used Rails. He wrote a Spring book, and he taught two weekend sessions 16 times per year for Hibernate.

- The Rails framework has some design philosophies that are unfamiliar to Java developers.

More importantly, some of the factors worked against Java in the implementation:

- The Java code was in no way fully tuned. The Java apps were much harder to tune, so we didn't get as far. We'd only started to look into performance. (The Ruby code was not fully tuned either, but its default implementation performs quite well with only some minor tweaks.)

- We had already implemented the problem once, so the Ruby implementation had the benefit of some experience. The dramatic difference in application structure tempers this somewhat, but the user interface was nearly identical.

- Justin did not have a chance to implement all possible tuning scenarios in all possible environments. The Java version used Tomcat on an Apple iBook instead of Resin or something faster. Justin just made a few simple tests.

- The caching models are fundamentally different, and are far easier to tune on Rails.

Still, with Ruby, we develop faster; we're probably four or five times as productive. Table 7-1 shows the raw productivity metrics. We write less code. There's less code to maintain. With this type of increase in our cycle time, the customer is much happier, and we can better react to last-minute changes. Our test code is every bit as rich, and probably more so.

Table 7-1. Productivity metrics

Metric	Java Spring/Hibernate	Ruby Rails
Time to market	4 months, approximately 20 hours/ week	4 nights (5 hours/night)
Lines of code	3,293	1,164
Lines of configuration	1,161	113
Number of classes/methods	62/549	55/126

Table 7-2 shows the performance numbers. They're probably a little more controversial. I'm not trying to show that a Ruby application will always be faster than a Java application. I'm just showing that in this case, Ruby is fast enough, and it took almost no time or experience to get to this point.

Table 7-2. Difference in performance between untuned versions of a Java application after we moved it to Ruby on Rails

Metric (requests per second)	Java Spring/Hibernate	Ruby Rails
User scenario 1 (100 runs) (no preexisting cache)	71.89	75.59
User scenario 1 (100 runs) (with preexisting cache)	80.86	174.39
User scenario 2 (100 runs) (no preexisting cache)	80.86	62.50
User scenario 2 (100 runs) (with preexisting cache)	88.97	1,785.15

To be clear, in no way is Justin claiming that we've done everything possible to tune the Java application. The point here is that tuning Rails to this level was nearly effortless, and tuning the Java examples requires much more skill, time, and effort. The Ruby version is fast enough to meet requirements, with very little additional effort.

The Community Response

When Justin published this experience, followed by supporting data across two blogs,* the Java community lashed out with surprising vigor. It's ironic, because Justin was completely honest with his numbers, and he presented performance numbers only after he was challenged by the community. You probably know that backlash will be particularly strong around disruptive technologies. In this case, the backlash may well be justified, because Rails is a credible threat to Java in some important niches, and it's likely to get stronger quickly. If Rails does happen, a whole lot of knowledge can get marginalized in a hurry.

Look, I'm not saying that this data is scientific, thorough, or even broadly applicable to other applications. It just reflects our experience, and as such, it is compelling. It tells me that Rails is productive, is fast enough to get the job done, generates less code, and is much easier to tune. The data does not prove but strongly suggests a few other hints as well. Rails could well be much more productive than Java for a pretty wide class of applications. Rails can handle sophisticated domains with inheritance and relationships. And Rails is often enough to get the job done.

Keep an open mind. Judge for yourself.

Rails by Example

The best way to understand Rails is to see it in action. Go to *http:// rubyforge.org* and download Ruby and RubyGems. (If you use the Windows one-click installer, you'll get RubyGems with that distribution.) If you don't already have one, download a relational database manager, too. I used MySQL. You'll begin to get the Rails experience at install time. RubyGems lets you install Ruby applications and their dependencies. At the command line, type:

```
gem install rails -v 0.12.1
```

Ruby will start the installation process. It goes up to RubyForge (*rubyforge. org*) and pulls down an index including the appropriate version of Rails and its dependencies. If you were to omit the version number, Ruby would get you the latest stable version. RubyGems will then prompt you for each dependency. Answer "Y," or answer "a" once for all dependencies:

```
Attempting remote installation of 'rails'
Updating Gem source index for: http://gems.rubyforge.org
```

---

* Justin Gehtland, Weblogs for Relevance, LLC (April 2005); *http://www.relevancellc.com/blogs. I *heart* rails*; *Some Numbers at Last*.

```
Install required dependency rake? [Yn]  Y
Install required dependency activesupport? [Yn]  Y
Install required dependency activerecord? [Yn]  Y
Install required dependency actionpack? [Yn]  Y
Install required dependency actionmailer? [Yn]  Y
Install required dependency actionwebservice? [Yn]  Y
Successfully installed rails, version 0.12.1
```

You'll notice that RubyGems will then attempt to build the documentation for each of the subcomponents and Rails. And that's it. Rails is installed. You're already getting hints about the approachability of Rails.

Generating a Basic Application

You can now generate a Rails project. Go to your working directory and ask Rails to generate a project called *trails*:

```
rails trails
```

Ruby creates a full directory structure that will contain your application. There's no guesswork, and all Rails projects will have a consistent format. I'll point out a few important directories:

app

This directory has your application code. You'll see a directory for each component of MVC and a couple of others.

config

This directory will be very light. You'll put in anything that needs special configuration, like the connection parameters for your database. Since Ruby makes excellent use of defaults, your *config* directory will stay sparse.

script

Your *trails* app comes with scripts that will help you generate code, and start your application server.

You'll notice a few other goodies as well, but for now, let's use one of the scripts to start Ruby's application server. Change to the *trails* directory, and type:

```
ruby script/server
```

If things are working, you'll see a server started on port 3000. You can go to *http://127.0.0.1:3000/* to make sure things are running. You'll get a Rails welcome message. You just started a development Ruby web server, configured for Rails. If you need to change some properties of the server, you'll just change the *script/server* script. Notice that Ruby programmers typically do configuration, like this server script, in Ruby scripts. You've already learned that Ruby handles structured data well, without XML. For example, this is the part of the *server* script that has the configuration options:

```
OPTIONS = {
  :port        => 3000,
  :ip          => "0.0.0.0",
  :environment => "development",
  :server_root => File.expand_path(File.dirname(__FILE__) + "/../public/"),
  :server_type => WEBrick::SimpleServer
}
```

This code simply defines a hash map called OPTIONS. The => operator maps keys on the lefthand side to values on the right. Nothing has really happened yet, but you should be paying attention. You've set up a whole lot of infrastructure in a very short time.

Our *trails* project will collect descriptions of mountain bike trails. We'll start simple, collecting an ID to go with a trail name, description, and difficulty. You'll type the field names once. The Rails metaprogramming features will read the columns from the database and dynamically add properties to your model objects. If you're using MySQL, you can fire up the mysql command processor. Create a database called *trails* and switch to it. Now, create a table called trails:

```
mysql> CREATE TABLE trails (
    ->     id int(6) NOT NULL auto_increment,
    ->     name varchar(20),
    ->     description text,
    ->     difficulty varchar(20),
    ->     primary key (id));
Query OK, 0 rows affected (0.36 sec)
```

Notice the names. They are important. By convention, if you're working with more than one row (as in a table or a list), the name should be a plural. A column or class that refers to a singular object should be singular. Rails is smart enough to translate English plurals, so it knows to create a model called Person for a table called people. Watch the capitalization in these examples, too. It's important. If you follow Rails conventions with your names, you can just stay with Rails defaults, and your code will be much more concise.

You'll need to tell Rails where to find your database. Edit *config/database. yml* to look like this:

```
development:
  adapter: mysql
  database: trails
  host: localhost
  username: root
  password: password
```

Stop and restart the server. (You only have to do so when you change your database configuration.) Let's generate a simple model. In the *trails* directory, simply type:

```
ruby script/generate model trail
```

Rails generates the model, some helper files, tests, and fixtures. For example, you can take a look at the model. Edit the file at *app/models/trail.rb*:

```
class Trail < ActiveRecord::Base
end
```

That certainly looks anticlimactic. It looks like you'll simply type custom code here, in hopes that Rails will generate the rest of the code somewhere else. But that's not what happens at all. At runtime, Rails will load the ActiveRecord base class. Rails will look at the name of the class and load the definition of a table called trails. Then, it will dynamically add attributes, getters, setters, and database access methods to the Trail base class! So, there's a lot more than meets the eye.

One of the scripts that Rails generates lets you manipulate your model from an irb session. Type:

```
ruby script/console
```

You can now easily manipulate your model. For example, you can say:

```
Trail.new do |trail|
  trail.name="Walnut Creek"
  trail.description="Meandering trail in Austin park"
  trail.difficulty="hard"
  trail.save
end
```

Now, you'll need a controller. You can generate that, too:

```
ruby script/generate controller trails
ruby script/generate model trails
```

You just created the model and a default controller in *app/controllers/trails_controller.rb* for a collective page of trails. When you edit it, the controller is empty. Make it look like this:

```
class TrailsController < ApplicationController
  def index
    render_text "This will be a trail someday..."
  end
end
```

Point your browser to the URL *http://localhost:3000/trail*. You'll see your message printed. Of course, you didn't learn Rails to print strings, so change your controller to this:

```
class TrailsController < ApplicationController
  scaffold :trails
end
```

scaffold is a method. The first parameter is :trails, a literal pointing to the Trails class. Save it, and load the same URL. Now, that's more interesting. You see a listing of trails. Click on the new trail link on the bottom. That's beyond interesting! You'll get a form like the one shown in Figure 7-1. You can see that the metaprogramming framework is working overtime. The scaffold method inferred the properties of the database and propagated them through the model and up to the user interface. You'll see exactly what goes into a scaffold controller later, but trust the magic for now.

Managing Relationships and Updating Views

A list of trails will not get you very far by itself. It's the interactions between objects that gets difficult. Say you want to access trails by their city. The first job is to generate the model for locations. First you'll need a database table:

```
mysql> CREATE TABLE locations (
    ->    id int(6) NOT NULL auto_increment,
    ->    city varchar(20),
    ->    state varchar(20),
    ->    primary key (id));
Query OK, 0 rows affected (0.35 sec)
```

Instead of dynamically generating the scaffolding, you can simultaneously generate the source code for the controller, and view, complete with scaffolding with ruby script/generate scaffold locations. Build the model for a single location with ruby script/generate model location. While you're at it, just to get a better look at what's going on behind the curtains, do the same for Trail with ruby script/generate scaffold trails. Look at what you've done by pointing your browser to *http://localhost:3000/locations*. Make sure it works, and add a few locations. I'm adding Austin, Texas, and Durango, Colorado.

It's time to write some code ourselves, instead of letting Rails do all the work. You're going to need to update your trails table to point to the right row in the new locations table. You'll do so by adding a new database column that points to location_id, like this:

```
alter table trails add location_id int(6);
```

You also need to tell Rails about the relationship. Modify the Trails model and the Location model to reflect the new relationships, like this:

```
class Trails < ActiveRecord::Base
  belongs_to :location
end

class Locations < ActiveRecord::Base
  has_many :trails
end
```

Figure 7-1. This application has less than 10 lines of code and configuration, because Rails inferred the structure from the database

A little description here is interesting. You've created a subclass of the ActiveRecord class in the Base module. You've then fired a method called belongs_to and passed it a symbol for the Locations class. This method will fire more metaprogramming code that actually adds the properties and methods to your code that will manage the relationships for you.

Next, you're going to have to edit the Trails view and controller to edit a location. The scaffolding created the new controllers and views under trails and locations, respectively.

It's time to modify some of the view code. The view code consists of HTML, with Ruby scripting mixed in, between the <% and %> tags. First, you'll need to make sure the view has all the information it needs. You'll do this in the edit method, in the controller. Change the edit method in *trails_controller. rb* to create a property called @locations that has all the locations:

```
class TrailsController < ApplicationController
  ...
  def edit
    @trail = Trail.find(@params[:id])
    @locations = Location.find_all
  end
  ...
end
```

It's also time to take over the full view that lets you edit a trail. You'll want the user to pick a location from a pick list with all possible locations. Change *app/views/trails/edit.rhtml* to look like this:

```
<html>
  <head><title>Edit a Trail</title></head>
  <body>
    <h1>Edit Trail</h1>

  <form action="../update" method="POST">
  <input id="trial_id" name="trail[id]" size="20"
        type="hidden" value="<%= @recipe.id %>" />
  <p><b>Name</b><br>
  <input id="trail_name" name="trail[name]" size="20"
        type="text" value="<%= @trail.name %>" />
  </p>
  <p><b>Location:</b><br>

  <%= collection_select("trail", "location_id", @locations, "id","city") %>

  <p><b>Description</b><br>
  <textarea cols="40" id="trail_description"
            name="trail[description]"
            rows="20" wrap="virtual">
    <%= @trail.description %>
  </textarea> </p>
  <input type="submit" value="Update" />
  </form>

  <a href="/trail/show/<%= @trail.id %>">
    Show
  </a> |
  <a href="/trail/list">
```

```
    Back
    </a>

    </body>
    </html>
```

As with most applications, your scaffolding won't hold up infinitely. Often you'll want to replace most of the view code. Rails lets you build toward the goal, instead of creating all of a model, view, and controller right off the bat.

Notice the code in bold. It adds an option value for all the locations (which you specified in the edit method of the controller), and selects the one that matches the one that reflects the model, shown in the variable trails. location.city.

Finally, you'll need to show the new data in the trail list, and in the show method. The idea is exactly the same. Add a line to the show.rhtml view right above the links on the bottom of the page:

```
<p>
  <b>Location:</b> <%=h @trail.location.city %>
</p>
```

That's pretty simple. You're just getting the location from the model passed in by the controller. The list view uses the same technique. You can edit the table from the app/views/trails/list view:

```
<table>
  <tr>
    <th>Name</th>
    <th>Location</th>
  </tr>

<% for trail in @trails %>
  <tr>
    <td><%= trail.name %></td>
    <td><%= trail.location.city %></td>
    <td><%= link_to 'Show', :action => 'show', :id => trail %></td>
    <td><%= link_to 'Edit', :action => 'edit', :id => trail %></td>
    <td><%= link_to 'Destroy', {:action => 'destroy', :id => trail}, :
confirm => "Are you sure?" %></td>
  </tr>
<% end %>
</table>
```

Figure 7-2 shows you the result, with the location of each trail in the main list. Keep in mind that all trails have to have locations. If one of yours doesn't, you will get an error here.

This tutorial has already gone on long enough, but I hope you can appreciate the power and flow of Rails development. You can quickly get your application rolling, because Rails discovers your application structure from

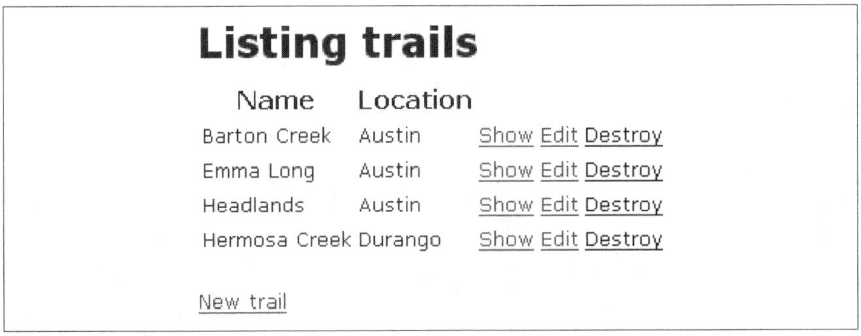

Listing trails

Name	Location			
Barton Creek	Austin	Show	Edit	Destroy
Emma Long	Austin	Show	Edit	Destroy
Headlands	Austin	Show	Edit	Destroy
Hermosa Creek	Durango	Show	Edit	Destroy

New trail

Figure 7-2. This list comes from an application that allows you to view and update a database, with trails in one table and locations in another

the database design. You then turn changes around quickly, because the feedback cycle requires you only to code/reload. You're building quality beyond what PHP can give you, because you're building with a proven model/view/controller design pattern, with built-in features for logging, caching, and automated testing. Now that you've seen what Rails can do, take a look under the hood to see some of this magician's secrets.

Under the Hood

As you've seen, the Rails framework is also made up of several existing frameworks, including Active Record, Action Pack, and a few others. Active Record handles relational database access. Action Pack processes requests, and manages the model/view/controller separation. Rails provides the integration and the rest.

Active Record

Active Record implements the Active Record design pattern by Martin Fowler in *Patterns of Enterprise Application Architecture* (Addison Wesley). It's effectively a wrapper around a database table, with domain logic built into the wrapper. The Rails implementation adds two important innovations: you can do inheritance and manage relationships. These are some of the major features.

Automatic properties

Active Record automatically adds properties, with accessors, to model objects. It also adds methods for simple CRUD database methods automatically. For example, in the view you just wrote, the view accesses the name property in Trail, though the root model was empty:

```
class Trail < ActiveRecord::Base
end
```

Association management

Rails uses methods to add methods that manage associations, automatically. You saw this example where a location has many trails:

```
class Location < ActiveRecord::Base
  has_many :trails
end
```

As you have seen, has_many is a method, and :trails is a symbol, in this case, for the Ruby class Trails.

Composition

You can use Active Record to compose objects from multiple tables, like this:

```
class Location < ActiveRecord::Base
  composed_of :street, :class_name => "Street",
              :mapping => %w(street name)
end
```

Inheritance

Inheritance works, putting all subclasses in a single table with the parents:

```
class Product < ActiveRecord::Base
end

class Bike < Product
end
```

Other features

Of course, a full Active Record discussion is beyond the scope of this book, but these are some of the other features you can use. You can build recursive relationships, like trees. You can use Active Record to validate certain types of rules (for instance, there must be an existing location for a new trail). Active Record can notify an email address when some significant event happens.

Active Record also has good plumbing. It supports transactions and error logging. You can look at the metadata for the columns for a table, and support multiple database types. It also provides support that makes it easy for you to build test fixtures. Active Record is a powerful framework and a credible competitor to Java's ORM frameworks.

Action Pack

Action Pack deals with requests in two parts: the controller and the view. Requests come into Action Pack through a dispatcher. The dispatcher routes the request to a controller, which invokes any model logic and sends the request to a template-driven view system. The template engine fires the Ruby template, which may execute Ruby code, and returns the resulting HTML to the browser. The flow, shown in Figure 7-3, is reminiscent of Struts. There are a few differences. For example, the controller has a group of actions, instead of encapsulating each action in a different class. If you wanted to refactor, you'd let actions share methods.

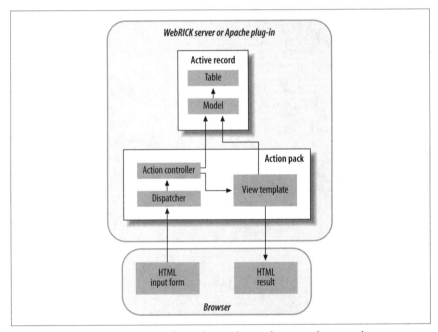

Figure 7-3. Ruby on Rails is actually made up of several existing frameworks, most notably Active Record and Action Pack

The Action Pack splits the request into a controller part and a view part. With Rails, a whole lot happens automatically. In some ways, that's bad. You can't see all the methods or the attributes on your class, and you don't even know what they are unless you look at the database. In other ways, it's a highly productive way to work. You can change your model, schema, and view in many cases just by adding columns to the schema. Let's take a fuller look at the capabilities of Action Pack.

Capabilities

Action Pack goes beyond simple request processing. It contains many capabilities that make it easier to develop web applications. I'll touch on some of the major capabilities here.

As you've seen, Action Pack uses Ruby as the scripting language. Java developers frown on embedding Java into a JSP, but I'd suggest that code will be in the view regardless of whether it's in Ruby. Early on, some vocal zealots overreacted to the early proliferation of Java scriptlets and decreed that MVC means "no code on the page." Many Ruby developers believe that code that is concerned with the view (and only the view) does belong on the page. Burying Java code in a custom tag only complicates and confuses the issue.

Ruby provides a far friendlier scripting language than JSTL tags, for example. Like servlets, Action Pack lets you attach filters for things like authentication. Action Pack also handles some convenience design elements, like automatically paginating your result sets and providing navigation links.

Action Pack also has some features that make it easier to build components, like helper classes (to render a date, for example), a layout sharing feature (similar to Tiles, if you're familiar with Struts), intracomponent communication, and pretty good Ajax integration. Like Struts and Spring, Action Pack provides good support for building and validating forms.

You'll need to manage your solution, and Action Pack builds in some features to help. It enables logging, caching at three levels (page, action, and fragment), and benchmarking support. Developers can use integrated support for unit testing and debugging. It's not as powerful as Struts in some ways, but it's much simpler, and highly customizable.

The Essence

So, Rails is not a toy, and it's not a gimmick. In my opinion, Rails represents a significant advance in the state of the art. You've probably seen frameworks like this one solve the database-with-UI problem in several different ways:

- Object-oriented development frameworks are flexible and robust. They're usually at a lower abstraction level, so they may not be as productive. You can use them to create flexible, robust, and powerful applications, but you're going to pay for it with productivity.

- Quick compromise frameworks trade conventional wisdom and sound design for implementation speed. PHP and Visual Basic, for example, compromise by trading design wisdom (frameworks should encourage separation of model and view logic) for development speed.

- Code generation frameworks generate most of the code for such an application at compile time. They trade the feedback cycle, easy maintenance, and often, customization, for speed.

- Customization point frameworks take a few parameters, like database tables or models, and build default implementations with a few well-defined anticipated customization points. These frameworks break down when the inventor's imagination doesn't anticipate important hook points.

Rails is none of these. It uses macros to help you quickly generate code based on the structure of the database and a few well-placed macros. Since you effectively get generated code at runtime without tangled source code, you don't have to maintain the added code. Rails avoids the trap of customization points through Ruby's extensive hook points. You start with a clean design. You can then extend it through subclassing, changing class definitions, or any of the other metaprogramming techniques we discussed. You can even replace major Rails components like Active Record.

Rails accelerates your development through meaningful conventions and defaults. By guiding your naming strategies in the database, Rails can save you lots of typing, and infer your intent by the consistent names that you provide.

Rails keeps development convenient by providing the scripts and debugging tools that you need to do the job right. You can run the server from a script, manage your active record classes and the database tables behind them from a console, use generated test fixtures, or run performance tests from generated scripts.

In *Hackers and Painters* (O'Reilly), Paul Graham suggested that great tools for good programmers are built by programmers to solve their own problems. I think he's on to something. Maybe Rails is so good because the authors built it to solve their own real-world problems first. As you've seen, Rails was created to help build the popular Base Camp and Back Pack projects.

Is Rails the Killer App?

Is Rails the catalyst that will take us beyond Java? I'm not sure. Ruby does not have strong commercial backing. There's no JVM implementation that will yet run Rails, and the existing project has had some false starts. Ruby doesn't have the rich frameworks or name recognition of Python and Java.

But it is an important advancement in productivity, in an important niche. And unlike Python, Groovy, and Lisp, Rails has generated an incredible buzz in the Java community right now. Something like Rails may be what eventually replaces Java in this web development niche.

Or Is Metaprogramming the Killer Technique?

On another level, Rails may use a killer technique. Rails is one of the first commercially successful demonstrations of metaprogramming in Ruby, in combination with meaningful defaults. Let's dive a little deeper into metaprogramming.

In some ways, this programming technique reminds me of another buzzword, the *domain specific language (DSL)*. A DSL solves a domain problem with a language whose syntax and keywords match ideas in the domain. Look over Active Record again. That framework lets you express ideas about the relationship between a database and a model, with keywords for ideas like inheritance, relationships, and name mappings.

Rails may be the application that breaks the dam. Some of my mentors, like Stuart Halloway and Glenn Vanderburg, speak often about the importance of these techniques. By showing what's possible in Ruby, Rails may release a massive wave of metaprogramming frameworks custom built for a given domain. If we do see such a wave, it likely won't be in Java, because reflection is just too painful, and the wild mix of primitives and objects simply makes it too cumbersome.

Final Thoughts on Ruby and Rails

To me, Ruby smells and feels like a good language, and Rails feels special. That alone is not enough to make it succeed. In this industry, individuals often make the difference, and the Davids (Thomas and Hansson) may be special enough to take this language and framework into the mainstream. Dave Thomas is a tireless promoter of all things pragmatic, and he seems to be focusing his publishing business on Ruby. He's already locked down many of the top Ruby authors by treating them well and providing a publishing experience that larger publishers cannot duplicate. Printed books provide credibility and exposure that languages need to succeed. David Heinemeier Hansson has a unique combination of a technical vision, a flair for understanding the end user, and a zest for marketing that you rarely find in one person. Rails is at once theoretically sound enough to attract hard-core web developers, and approachable enough to attract the masses.

This kind of leadership often makes the difference between a successful technology, and a good technology that failed or never hit the mainstream. You don't often find technical passion and marketing vision wrapped up in a single mind, but when you do, great things can happen. Bill Gates built Microsoft from a BASIC shop operating out of a garage to the biggest software company in the world. Steve Jobs made Apple cool, left, and came back to overhaul its image and bring it back. Java, too, is full of technical visionaries. James Duncan Davidson fought the bureaucracy in Sun to break servlets into the mainstream by open sourcing Tomcat, and then did it again with Ant.

Java seems to be losing the visionaries and technologists that I respect the most. Glenn Vanderburg may pay some of his bills with Java, but his public persona now spends more time in the Smalltalk (Seaside) and Ruby communities, because of his interest in metaprogramming. James Duncan Davidson left the Java community years ago to focus on the Apple operating system, primarily on Objective C. Many of those who remain seem to be here because Java pays the bills.

Ruby and Rails seem to be going in the other direction. Increasingly, Rails finds itself in the middle of controversy. You've probably heard all the arguments:

- Can it possibly scale?
- Is it ready for the enterprise?
- What will you do without all of those Java programmers and libraries?
- Isn't Rails a toy?
- Do you really want to run your business on a scripting language?

In the first half of 2005, I saw more than two dozen blogs attacking Rails. Some of the arguments are valid. Java can do some things that Ruby can't, yet. Other arguments are born out of ignorance or misconceptions. I'm intrigued, because more and more in the Java community are paying attention. The Davids certainly get the Rails message out there. We're about to see whether that spotlight will provide energy for growth, or a sweltering, destructive, withering heat.

CHAPTER 8

Continuation Servers

I rarely run rapids on blind faith. If there's any danger, I like to know exactly what the water and rocks could do to me, and I need a plan to deal with any potential trouble. On this day, though the consequences for failure were high, the move was easy. I still don't know exactly how it worked, but I watched boater after boater thrust, brace, and arrive in the turbulent boil below *The Elbow*, a slotted 20-foot drop that guidebooks describe as a deadly entrapment motel. Sure, I could tell you that the move was called a slot move, and I'd need to apply my brace with perfect timing and angle to avoid hitting the wall on the way down. I knew the timing, because I'd been told. It's just the "why" of it that was a mystery. The experts tried to tell me why it worked. Most really didn't know. No one could really tell me with any kind of certainty how the rocks were configured at the bottom. They just knew that at this river level, the move worked. And so it did.

At different points in my programming life, a few tricks held the same kind of mystery for me: recursion as a college student, my first glimpse at reflection shortly thereafter, and now, continuation servers. In this chapter, you'll see continuations, and how they're used in a new class of application servers.

The Problem

Web development, for all its usefulness, often happens with a curious inelegance. It's kind of like making sausage. I like the result, but I don't want to see how it's made. Web programming in Java was better than web programming in alternative languages. It gave you more structure with easier maintenance and, often, better scalability than Visual Basic or Perl-based approaches, and an easier programming model than C++. But for all the benefits, certain problems make it seem clunky and awkward.

What You Want

Current web application servers might be powerful, but they're not convenient or natural. So, what is convenient and natural? It shouldn't take too much effort to figure that out. What if your controllers looked like this:

```
if (logon.show( ) == true) {
  mainPage.show( );
}
```

or this:

```
if (shoppingCart.verify( )) checkout.show( );
```

That's better. What you really want to do is encapsulate the presentation of one or more web screens in a method. Then, more sophisticated page flows would not be a problem. You could simply roll up more and more pages into higher-level components. For example, you could take this code:

```
checkoutAddress.showForm( );
if(checkoutAddress.getSeparateBilling) checkoutBilling.showForm( );
creditCardNumber.showForm( );
```

and roll it up onto a method:

```
public static void showCheckoutWizard( ) {
  checkoutAddress.showForm( );
  if(checkoutAddress.getSeparateBilling) checkoutBilling.showForm( );
  creditCardNumber.showForm( );
}
```

so the usage becomes:

```
cart.showCheckoutWizard( );
```

in its cleaner, refactored form. But you can't code that way, because your web server won't let you. Creators of most web application servers will sell their soul to keep things stateless and scalable.

Statelessness

Think of living without any short-term memory. Normal conversations in day-to-day life would be nearly impossible. Think of the logistics:

- You'd have to write down every important phrase of every conversation as it occurred.

- Then, when someone asked you a question, you'd have to look up the history of your conversation with that person before you could answer.

- To optimize things, you'd have to decide how much information you should keep close by—say, in your briefcase—versus at home, in your filing cabinets.

- When information got too old, you'd need to throw it out.

- You'd have to maintain this whole system and revisit it when it didn't meet your needs.

That's the status quo for web developers. Your briefcase is the HTTP session, and your file cabinet at home is the relational database. It's an insane proposition, but we deal with the tedium because the Web is so important, and stateless solutions scale better. So, you willingly take a pretty large stride away from the ideal solution. Still, each time you struggle with the awkward little edge cases, you ask yourself if there's a better way, some kind of abstraction that fits the problem more neatly.

The Back Button

Saving state within simple conversations does not cover the whole problem. On the Web, conversations are not linear. Users can and do change their minds, pressing the Back button. Some assumptions that you've made as you continue to accumulate data may no longer apply.

Sometimes, you'll want to keep the user from going back, such as when she's made a purchase, or done something to force a committed change in a relational database. In these cases, you can simply punt and disable the Back button. Most often, you need to build special support for the Back button. You may even have to remove data from a database that a user would not have seen yet. Worse, many web designers simply don't solve the problem, and tell the user to expect unintuitive behavior. You've taken one more step back, away from the ideal. Once again, this awkward Back button forces you to deal with things on a case-by-case basis, and it just doesn't feel right.

Navigation

Web development in Java focuses an incredible amount of brain power around navigation and flow. You'd think controlling flow from the server side would be natural, but servers can't update clients—they can only respond to requests. This simple little truism forces servers to handle hundreds of little requests rather than a couple dozen application flows. It's also hard to synchronize the user interface with the model. You'd like to use a simple method call that controls the user interface and model, but you can't. The web server just doesn't work that way. And you're stepping back again, and you've got that sinking suspicion that there's a cliff behind you somewhere.

Continuation Servers to the Rescue

A new class of web servers called continuation servers is starting to make some real noise. A continuation server uses a programming construct called the *continuation* to keep enough information about a request to be able to completely reconstruct the context. In technical terms, a continuation saves the execution environment, including the call stack. In practical terms, using continuations in a web server lets the server maintain context for you, freeing you to program in a more natural way.

Continuations

You've probably played video games. Think of a continuation as a *save game* feature. As you're playing your game, you save your current game. You can feel free to take your chances with the monster control center. If you die, you simply restore the game. Said another way, a continuation is a snapshot of a point in time. Continuations let you save the system's state (in the form of an execution stack) in one place, and then return to that state on command.

Since I've already introduced Ruby's syntax, I'll first show you continuations in Ruby, where continuation syntax is clean and precise. Then, I'll show you Seaside, the most popular continuation-based server, in Smalltalk.

In Ruby, a code block defines the universe for the continuation. You'll use a continuation object to hold the execution state, consisting of the execution stack. You'll later invoke a call method on the continuation object to restore the system state, replacing the current execution state, including the call stack, with the one in the continuation object. The call returns execution to the point immediately after the code block. From Ruby's perspective, you're conceptually letting your execution state jump back in time.

The Syntax

In Ruby, you get a continuation by calling the `callcc` method on `Kernel` and passing it a code block. This block does nothing with the continuation but print its object identifier:

```
irb(main):001:0> callcc {|continuation| puts continuation}
#<Continuation:0x28c2dd8>
```

This passive little program does more than you think it does. The argument called `continuation` is a powerful little gem that has the whole execution context, with variable values and the entire call stack, at the time that you called `callcc`. Look at it as a saved game, or a frozen moment in time. You can return to that moment in time. Specifically, Ruby will return to execute the statement immediately after the continuation block by calling the continuation. Here's a trickier continuation example:

```ruby
callcc do |continuation|
  for i in 1..10 do
    continuation.call if (i == 7)
    puts i
  end
  puts 'This never happens.'
end
puts 'Good bye.'
```

And the output:

```
>ruby forloop.rb
1
2
3
4
5
6
Good bye.
>
```

Once again, the whole `callcc` statement is a point in time. When i is 7, Ruby executes `continuation.call`. That takes control to the point right after the continuation code block, so the last two numbers don't get printed, and the `puts 'This never happens.'` in fact doesn't happen. The `callcc` method loads the application stack in the continuation, abruptly sending execution to the line of code immediately after the continuation code block, or `puts 'Good bye.'`. It moves execution around a little bit like a goto.

Of course, you'd not usually use continuations to break out of a for loop. Continuations take on a little more power when you pass them out of the code block, such as with a method call.

A More Powerful Example

Keep in mind that the continuation will return the call stack and local variables in the block to the way they were when you made the continuation call. So, this program:

```ruby
1  def loop
2    for i in 1..5 do
3      puts i
4      callcc {|continuation| return continuation} if i==2
5    end              # cont.call returns here
6    return nil
7  end
8
```

```
 9  puts "Before loop call"
10  cont=loop()
11  puts "After loop call"
12  cont.call if cont
13  puts "After continuation call"
```

gives you this result:

```
>ruby continuation.rb
Before loop call
1
2
After loop call
3
4
5
After loop call
After continuation call
```

So, we were able to exit the loop when something happened and return to the loop on command. Since continuations are so alien, let's look at this example in a little more detail. It's not too bad to read, once you know what's happening. Line 4 saves the game, putting it into a container. Line 12 restores the game. Let's break it down a little further, thinking like a Ruby interpreter:

- Start on line 9, after the method declaration.
- Execute line 9, printing the string Before loop call.
- Execute line 10, calling the method called loop. Put line 10 on the call stack, so you'll remember where to return after the method call.
- Enter the method loop, specified in line 1.
- Do the first pass through the for loop in lines 2-5. i has a value of 1. You'll print 1.
- Start the second pass through the for loop. i now has a value of 2. You'll print 2.
- At line 4, i is 2, so make the callcc call in three steps. First, make a copy of the call stack. Second, make a copy of the instance variables (i is 2). Third, push the line after the continuation block (line 5) onto the *copy* of the call stack, so now the continuation's copy of the stack has (line 5, line 10). The call stack simply has (line 10).
- At line 4, execute the return statement. You'll return the value of continuation to the line on the top of the call stack. The call stack has line 10, so you'll return the value of continuation to line 10. Set cont to the returned continuation. Recall the continuation has the current execution context—the call stack has (line 5, line 10), and variable i has a value of 2.

- Execute line 11, printing the screen `After call loop`.
- Execute line 12. Calling the continuation restores the execution state. Set the value of `i` to 2. Go to the line number on the top of the call stack so that you'll remove it from the call stack. Now the call stack has only line 10.
- Execute the rest of the `for` loop, for `i=3`, 4, and 5.
- You'll return `nil`. The call stack has 10 on it, so you'll return to line 10, and assign `cont` to `nil`.
- Execute lines 13 and 15. Skip line 14 because `cont` is `nil`.

This continuation example shows you a few nice capabilities. You can take a snapshot of execution state at some point in time, like we did within the `for` loop. You can save that execution state in an object, as we did in the `cont` object. You can then return to the execution state stored in a continuation object at any point.

Why Would You Use Them?

You might first think that continuations are the most useful when you want to break logical control structures, as in implementing a break for our `for` loop, or processing exceptions. For the most part, though, you want to think "suspend and resume." Continuations are marvelous in these kinds of scenarios. Cooperative multitasking lets one program voluntarily relinquish control to another application, and resume at a later date. This problem is remarkably easy to solve using continuations. A subtler use involves communication. When you've got an application that spans multiple computers with synchronous request/response communication, you often want to suspend control until the remote system responds. When you need to scale this solution, suspending control while you wait frees the system to handle other requests. The system can conveniently resume your application without disruption when the remote system responds, simply by calling a continuation.

Continuation Servers

You can probably begin to see why continuations might be interesting for web servers. If you want to look at a web application as one continuous application with suspend/resume breaks in between to communicate with the user, it makes more sense. While waiting for user input in the form of an HTTP request, the web server could simply store a state, stash the continuation object away in the HTTP session, and instantly return to that frozen point in time when it's time to process another request. Notice in Figure 8-1 that I've conveniently inverted the control. Instead of thinking of a web app as a series of request/response pairs initiated by the user, I can think of a web app as a series of response/request pairs controlled by the server. My server code gets much simpler.

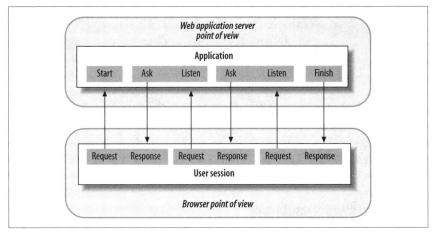

Figure 8-1. Continuation servers invert control from client to server, simplifying the world view, and the code, of the server

Your web application server is no longer composed of many different independent requests. The server can conveniently look at the world as a bunch of simple end-to-end applications. It processes individual requests by loading the state of each user when it's time to process another request, and suspending the user's application when it's time to communicate with the user again. *Voilá!* Your application can maintain state, and use it to seamlessly control application flow.

At a lower level, the continuation server becomes a collection of web applications with states frozen at a point in time, in the form of continuations. Each user has a session. The continuation server assigns an ID to each session, and organizes the continuations per session. After each request, the continuation server takes a snapshot of the execution state with a continuation object, and associates that continuation with the session. So, a server has multiple sessions, and each session has one or more continuations representing frozen points in time, as shown in Figure 8-2. You can no longer see individual HTTP requests, because they're buried in the application flow. As they should be!

Glenn Vanderburg: Continuation Servers

Author of *Maximum Java 1.1*

Glenn Vanderburg, a consultant from Dallas, has been writing Java programs since before it was called Java, and was the author of one of the first advanced Java books. Glenn has 19 years of software development experience, encompassing a wide variety of languages, platforms, industries, and domains.

What's wrong with current web development models, like the Servlet model?

GV: There are two big problems. I'll start with the most obvious. When I did mainframe programming, I would build a screen of information mixed with form fields, and push it out to a 3270 terminal. The program wouldn't hear from the terminal again until the user hit Enter. Sound familiar?

In the mainframe days, the program got to pause and wait on the user's submission. Web programming is actually worse, because in the interest of scaling to thousands of users (as opposed to hundreds), the program is asked to forget as much as possible between each interaction so that each submission can stand alone. The stateless nature of the web programming model forces programmers to manually manipulate, store, and retrieve the program state at every stage. Web frameworks help some, but programmers still have to consider carefully how to deal with each piece of state. One mistake and we get web applications that are (at best) very confusing to use.

The other big deficiency of the web development model is that our programs are held together with strings. The navigational structure is defined by URLs we stick in links, and those URLs have to also go in configuration files to tie them to pieces of code that get invoked. User input comes to us in form fields that are named with strings. State that we store in the session is usually referenced by a key that is a string. We have all of these strongly typed programming languages and IDEs to go with them to make sure we don't make silly errors like misspelling variable names, but that all goes out the window with web apps, because the tools don't help us to validate all of our uses of URL fragments, form fields, etc. Also, those strings provide ways for crackers to attack our applications. Here again, some frameworks help us manage the tangled ball of strings, but most of them just reduce the problem, they don't solve it.

| *But those fundamental problems come straight from HTTP and HTML, not Java, right?* | **GV:** True, but we shouldn't discount how much they hurt our productivity. Those two things together make web applications significantly more complex than more traditional counterparts. And complexity costs us—in time and in quality. Managing the complexity of our systems is the fundamental problem of software development. |

What is a continuation server?

GV: First, I really don't like the term *continuation server*, for two reasons. First, it obscures what these servers and frameworks are all about. They serve web applications. Frameworks like Seaside and Iowa employ continuations as a way of hiding the stateless, back-and-forth nature of web applications from the programmer. Continuations are used deep inside the framework; developers don't deal with them directly. The second reason I don't really like the term is that continuations are just one of the techniques that frameworks like Seaside use to provide a better web development experience.

What these servers do is to use continuations (as well as closures stored as callbacks, plus automatic tracking of session state and caching of backtracking information) to build high-level abstractions for web development, transparently handling many of the messy details that web developers are constantly wrestling with. Continuations, closures, and the common features of dynamic languages provide much more powerful tools for abstraction than Java does.

What do they bring to the table?

GV: They simplify web development. And it's a radical simplification: many of the most difficult issues of web development, things that nearly all applications punt on because they're too difficult, are handled automatically and transparently so that they're built into your applications by default. Seaside, for example, makes it easy to develop web applications that work the way users expect: proper handling of the Back button, proper session forking if the user opens multiple windows or tabs, and no "accidental double purchase" when backing up to a form result page.

In Seaside, web application code looks like the code you'd write for a desktop application. Need to ask the user a question? Call a dialog, wait for it to return, and act on the result. Of course, within the scope of that dialog call, a lot of things happen: a continuation is saved, a dialog page is sent to the browser, the user considers the question (possibly for a long time) and answers, and when Seaside receives the response it looks up the saved continuation, calls it—and the dialog call returns, just as if the thread had been waiting on the response the whole time. And, in a very lightweight sense, it actually was.

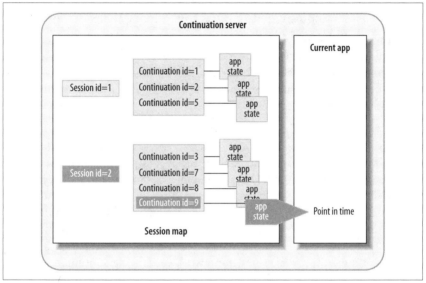

Figure 8-2. A continuation server stores snapshots that have the state of web applications in progress

Advantages and Disadvantages

You've seen the primary benefit: you can look at a web application as one big piece, instead of coordinating lots of little requests. That's incredibly powerful. Continuation servers have some other capabilities as well. The Back button problem becomes much easier to solve, because if the Back button is not disabled, you can just revert the application state to the last continuation, *or any previous continuation*. To disable the Back button, you simply tell the browser and delete past continuations. Threading also becomes trivial, because each thread can work on a private continuation, each with an application's own resources. You don't have to worry about serializing access to a shared session.

Continuation servers work best for applications that have complex state management issues and sophisticated control flows between pages. The continuation server simplifies navigation dramatically by letting you maintain application state between pages.

Continuation servers do have a few problems:

- The servers typically attach identifiers to URLs, and some don't like ugly URLs (though web sites like Amazon.com use them).

- You must guarantee *session affinity*, meaning that after an initial request in a user's session, the same machine must serve the user for every subsequent request. You could overcome this problem with a distributed continuation cache, but just as distributed HTTP sessions are a problem, distributing a continuation cache may not be completely practical.

- Continuations are more expensive than other session management techniques. I've seen little practical evidence that this has been a problem in production deployments. Still, some believe this approach will not scale as well as traditional web apps. Research on partial continuations will probably solve this problem eventually.

To me, the powerful advantages dwarf the potential disadvantages. It's possible, even likely, that a continuation server in some language will garner enough popularity to serve as a catalyst. Respected programmers Dave Thomas, Glenn Vanderburg, and David Heinemeier Hansson have all pointed to the continuation server as an important technology to watch. *Hackers and Painters* author, Paul Graham, used continuations in web applications with devastating effect at Viaweb, on an application that eventually became Yahoo! Store. He's also a proponent of continuation servers. Let's see an example of the most popular web framework supporting continuations.

Seaside

Seaside is a highly productive web development framework written in Smalltalk. Avi Bryant initially developed Seaside in Ruby, in a framework called Iowa. Early Ruby continuations had a few problems, so the original author of Seaside moved to Smalltalk. Since then, he's been improving the framework and using it to deliver commercial applications. Seaside has a few defining characteristics:

- Seaside renders HTML programmatically. Most Java frameworks render HTML with templates. I don't know enough to advocate one method over another, but it's certainly different, and it works well in Seaside's model.

- Seaside has a model for components. A Seaside component manages user interface state and renders itself in HTML. Seaside components are highly reusable, and they let you think in increments smaller than a page.

- Seaside makes it easy to manage a link. You can specify a link with a code block, so links don't get out of sync. The framework manages them for you.

- Seaside is modal. This is the author's word for a continuation server approach. Seaside lets you express one web page, or multipage web flows, in a single method.

- Seaside's debugging is the best I've ever seen. From within the browser, you can open a web-based Smalltalk browser, complete with code. You can also inspect the values of all the objects in the application.

Of course, you also get the advantages of using a highly dynamic language. You get a rapid feedback loop, interactive interpretation as needed, and full access to Smalltalk's excellent environments. I used the Squeak IDE for examples in this chapter. Squeak is a dialect of Smalltalk popularized by Disney.

A Little Smalltalk Syntax

Before we get too far, you should know a little Smalltalk syntax. Don't worry. I'm not saying that Smalltalk is the next great language; I just want you to see the power of the best continuations-based server. If you want to follow along, download the Squeak IDE from *http://www.squeak.org/ download/index.html*. Start Squeak, click on Tools, and drag a workspace and transcript window onto your desktop. Use your workspace window for input, and look to the transcript window for output.

Smalltalk syntax is quite simple. Type an object name first, the method second, and any parameters third. Let's evaluate a few statements. In your workspace, type:

```
Transcript show: 'Hello'
```

Highlight it, right-click, and then select do it from the menu. (You can also use Alt-D before you press Enter, to evaluate the line.) You should see the word *Hello* in your Transcript window. Transcript is the object, show: is the method (Smalltalk calls methods *messages*), and 'Hello' is a parameter.

Like Ruby, Smalltalk supports code blocks, though the syntax is a little different. Evaluate this:

```
1 to: 5 do: [:i | Transcript show: i]
```

First, you see that [and] mark the beginning and end of the code block. i is a parameter for the code block. In the declaration, you'll precede it with a colon.

Let's try multiple statements. Smalltalk terminates statements with a period. Logic uses messages and code blocks:

```
age := 4.
(age > 16)
    ifFalse: [Transcript show: 'Youngster.']
    ifTrue: [Transcript show: 'Old timer.']
```

This bit of code sets age to 4 with the := message. Then, it sends the ifFalse: method to the (age > 16) expression. The first code block is a parameter for ifFalse, and gets called if the expression evaluates to false.

You can see the influence of the elegance of Smalltalk in Java, and other languages, too. Java's garbage collection, design patterns, and collections all share Smalltalk's influence. Consider Hibernate's use of message chaining. If a method doesn't have a return value, it simply returns itself, enabling tighter code like this:

```
cfg.add("pet.hbm")
    .add("vet.hbm")
    .add("pet.hbm");
```

Many ideas from Eclipse have roots in IBM's VisualAge for Java, which first shared IDE code and a virtual machine with a Smalltalk product. Smalltalk syntax is wonderfully consistent.

A Seaside Overview

Seaside is a Smalltalk framework and a server. Remember, a continuation server is different from other web servers, so Seaside must run in its own environment. In Squeak, you'll left-click on the desktop to give you a menu (called the *world menu*). Then, you'll select Open... → SqueakMap Package Loader. Use it to install four packages: DynamicBindings, KomServices, KomHttpServer, and Seaside, in that order. Now, your Smalltalk image has Seaside. To see it, fire up the server. In Squeak, you'll open a workspace and evaluate:

```
WAKom startOn: 9090
```

WAKom is the name of the server. starton: is a method that tells the server to start on a supplied port, 9090 in this case. In some ways, WAKom is like Tomcat, or any other web application server. You can configure it by pointing your browser to:

```
http://localhost:9090/seaside/config
```

You'll see Seaside's configuration screen. Some of the items should look familiar to you. You'll see a list of registered applications, and some configuration options. Later, it will become clear that Seaside is more than Tomcat in Java.

A Seaside Example

Under the /seaside heading, notice the list of apps. One of the examples that you see in the configuration screen is store. Click on it. You'll see Sushi-Net, one of the more bizarre examples for web frameworks. In the search window, type the word Tuna. Click on two different tunas to add them to your cart. Now click the Back button and notice that you go back to a previous page, just the way it was. Add another tuna to your cart, and you'll notice that the old tuna item is still in your cart. So, you can override the Back button behavior, as needed.

Components

Notice the three boxes across the top of the screen, in Figure 8-3. Seaside is a component-based architecture. Each component has independent rendering, and each has a model behind it.

Figure 8-3. This Seaside application has three major components, each with independent rendering and business logic

This component-oriented approach often makes it much easier to design and refactor complex web screens. For example, here's the rendering for the shopping cart:

```
html divNamed: 'cart' with: [
  html small: [html bold: 'Your cart:'].
  html table: [
    cart countsAndItems do:
    [:assoc | self renderRowForCount:
              assoc key of: assoc value on: html ].
```

```
html spacerRow.
html
  tableRowWith: ''
  with: ''
  with: [html bold: cart totalPrice printStringAsCents].
]
```

Notice that Seaside components have code that generates HTML. Java people don't tend to like this approach either, but it's very productive in Seaside. The code in bold generates the table. First, you see the table message passed to the html object. This will generate table tags around the code block. Next, you'll see a loop that processes the items in the cart, a spacer row, and a row with the totals.

Complex Control Flows

For this application, the most complex series of windows is the checkout. Think of how a traditional stateful application would manage the flow of control. Try out the checkout in the application and see how it works. Add a few pieces of sushi to your cart and click on Checkout. This piece of Sushi-Net will walk you through a few major steps:

- You'll verify the contents of your cart. If you like your order, you can click "Proceed with checkout." Otherwise, you'll click "Modify my order." So the user makes a decision, and flow changes based on the user's input.

- You'll specify a shipping address. You can then choose whether to use this address for your billing address. Again, this decision impacts the flow of the application. If you don't want to use the same address for shipping and billing, SushiNet will reuse the component that renders the shipping address for the billing addresses. Nice.

- You'll enter your credit card information. If it doesn't verify, you'll go back to the same screen. If it does verify, you'll get a success screen.

- Users can click the Back button at any time. If the user hits the Back button after his order is submitted, he'll get a message that the page has expired.

So, the flow looks something like Figure 8-4. It's not that complicated. You've got four decisions, and based on the decisions, you route the user to the appropriate place.

If you implemented this flow with Java servlets, you'd need to process four or more independent requests, as in Figure 8-5. Each one would have to first load the current state at the beginning of a request, and store the current state at the end of the request. The web flow would be based on the user's

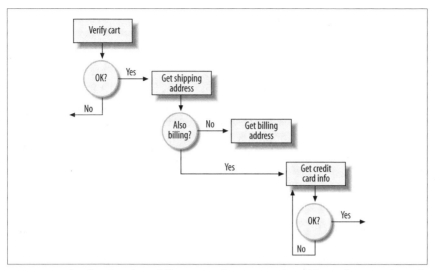

Figure 8-4. This flow has three different user decisions, and would complicate traditional web apps

decisions, so you'd have several forwards. Changes in flow would lead to potentially major refactoring.

Figure 8-5. Java servlets view the checkout problem as four or more independent requests

With a continuations approach, the logic becomes almost trivial, as you see in Figure 8-6. You can simply look at the flow as one simple component, called Checkout. That component can handle flows involving more than one component, or more than one page! The code looks seductively simple.

Figure 8-6. With Seaside and other continuation servers, the flow becomes a single, integrated method

Debugging and browsing

Since you have a frozen continuation, it's easy for Seaside to provide a complete snapshot of the execution state. Seaside goes a step further and gives you access to a web-enabled browser. At the bottom of the screen, you should see a few links. Seaside creates them by default for all the applications. Notice that you can do profiling or check memory usage, but I've got something else in mind. Click on the link called Toggle Halos.

You should see a frame with three icons appear around each component. These icons give you a full code browser, an inspector, and a cascading style sheet editor. Click on the browser icon (the first one). Notice that you can see exactly where the execution state is frozen. Next, click on (from left to right) Seaside-Examples-Store, WAStoreTask, and Go. You see the code for the store task.

You'll see the code that implements the cart in Figure 8-4:

```
go
  | shipping billing creditCard |
  cart _ WAStoreCart new.
  self isolate:
    [[self fillCart.
    self confirmContentsOfCart]
      whileFalse].

  self isolate:
    [shipping <- self getShippingAddress.
     billing <- (self useAsBillingAddress: shipping)
                   ifFalse: [self getBillingAddress]
                   ifTrue: [shipping].
     creditCard <- self getPaymentInfo.
     self shipTo: shipping billTo: billing payWith: creditCard].

  self displayConfirmation.
```

Tasks

In Seaside, tasks handle business logic. Let's zero in on the code in bold. It handles everything after the cart verification. The self isolate method takes a code block and makes sure everything in the block is an atomic operation, or a transaction. The next line of code is interesting:

```
[shipping <- self getShippingAddress.
```

This statement actually presents the getShippingAddress web page to the user, and puts the resulting address into the shipping address. You can see how the framework inverts control. Now, instead of the browser being in control, Seaside lets you direct traffic from the server. The next three lines show a decision:

```
billing <- (self useAsBillingAddress: shipping)
              ifFalse: [self getBillingAddress]
              ifTrue: [shipping].
```

The `useAsBillingAddress` method presents the decision screen. The expression (`self useAsBillingAddress: shipping`) returns a Boolean, and will trigger either the `ifFalse:` or `ifTrue:` methods. `ifFalse:` will actually trigger the code block [`self getBillingAddress`], which sends yet another web page to the user.

Though the Smalltalk syntax may seem awkward, if you're a Struts or Servlet developer, you're probably smiling right now. This approach frees you to work at higher abstractions. You can roll up several components, or pages, into a single task, and the continuation server keeps the management simple. State and navigation issues just melt away.

So What?

I'm pretty sure that continuation servers will prove to be important. I'm equally sure that Seaside is not a killer app that will suddenly spring Smalltalk into the mainstream. Smalltalk has 30 years of reputation to overcome. In this time, Smalltalk has rarely been more than an academic language with small forays into commercial development. The Smalltalk community is smart and has technical vision, but I've not yet seen the marketing leadership that will break Smalltalk into the mainstream. After 30 years, that's not likely to change.

Continuation servers do have some minor hurdles to overcome:

- So far, the servers require ugly, temporary URLs, because each continuation must have a unique identifier. Users don't like uglier URLs. Like Amazon, Seaside works around this limitation by providing a meaningful piece of the URL, followed by the continuation ID.

- Continuation servers will not scale as well, because saving continuations is stateful and expensive, though if you think about it, the problem is not quite as bad as it could be. Most of the continuations in a server will have common code for the framework. Only the last part of the call stack should be different from one continuation to the next. Partial continuations should provide a good performance boost.

- So far, the best servers are on academic languages. Lisp, Smalltalk, and Ruby may be holding them back. And of course, continuation servers may help break one of those languages closer to the mainstream.

Still, in the end, continuation servers will play a role, because they're a much more natural and powerful abstraction, and they represent a much more natural way to program. Systems continually get more processing power, and both short-term and long-term storage get cheaper. Productivity eventually trumps all else. In the end, continuation servers are fast enough. Higher abstractions make us more productive. If you held a gun to my head and forced me to make a prediction, I'd guess that continuation servers will evolve and break into the mainstream, but not on Java, or a derivative like C#. Such a language would have to simulate continuations. The concept is cleanest and purest when it is implemented on a more dynamic, higher-level language. I'd guess that continuation servers, in a language like Python or Ruby, may well prove to provide the foundation for all web application servers, in some not-too-distant future.

CHAPTER 9

Contenders

It was my first Class IV river, and I approached the infamous Five Falls. In the typically tame Ouachita mountain range, the *Cassatot*—Indian for Skull Crusher—was serious. In all honesty, I wasn't ready for the river. Unseen gremlins sent massive jets and waves of water shooting through the waterfalls and toyed with me, smashing my boat against rocks, turning me around, and flipping me over at will. Yet, my guide seemed in complete harmony with every molecule of the river. He harnessed all the power the rapids threw at him, and danced his boat across the many chutes, waves, and even face of the waterfall known as the Washing Machine.

Throughout the run, every inch of my body hurt as I learned to push off my foot braces to integrate the rarely used leg muscles into every stroke, because on this particular river, I needed all the leverage I could get. At the takeout, exhausted, I slithered out of my boat. My guide hobbled out of his boat, and I couldn't speak. Both of his legs were amputated above his knees. I was stunned. He was able to do everything on the river without the added balance and power that two legs would have given him. Those few seconds completely changed my perception about what was possible in a kayak. More than any other, that moment shaped my paddling. Since I know how far I can come, I've always been looking for ways to use the boat, paddle, body, and river to do more work with less effort.

If nothing else, this book is about changing perceptions. Sure, the Java libraries have legs—libraries and community. But the community can be dysfunctional at times, and the culture is leading to increasingly complex libraries. The JCP seems to be getting in the way, valuing politics and committees more than good libraries hardened in the crucible of experience. There's something to be said for a fresh start on a stronger foundation.

So, don't let Java's built-in advantages always lead you to sell the alternatives short. They've come a long way. In this chapter, I'll touch on the major contenders and some also-rans.

The Primary Contenders

So far, I've taken an in-depth look at one language and two application development models. I just don't have the time or will to do a comprehensive treatment of languages, but this book wouldn't be complete without at least mentioning some of the major alternatives. I'll take a longer look at what I see as the major alternatives. Then, I'll mention a few alternatives that I see as less likely.

I've got a few things working against me. I like short books, so there's not enough time to do a remotely comprehensive treatment. Even if I were inclined to do so, my practical experience is limited to some Ruby, a little Smalltalk, and a few lines of Lisp in college. I'm just one Java developer, who's prejudging the overall landscape based on my limited experience. In my favor are my broad and diverse network, an excellent set of reviewers, good access to corporate opinions at major vendors and customers, and a strong track record of predicting successful technologies.

Instead of picking a winner, I'd just like to lay out the factors in favor of a language, and those against. In such a short treatment of this problem, I'm not going to be able to do any remotely complete treatments of any given language, but based on Java's history and this community, I should be able to give you a good sense of what's important.

Steve Yegge: Python, Ruby, and Groovy
Language expert and creator of Wyvern

Steve Yegge, a graduate of the University of Washington, spent five years as an Assembly-language programmer at Geoworks and more than six years as a software development manager at Amazon.com. Steve somehow managed to find time to design, implement, and maintain a massive multiplayer game called Wyvern (http://www.cabochon.com/), with a half-million lines of Java and Python code.

What do you think of Ruby and Python?

SY: They're both amazingly expressive, easy to learn, and easy to read. They're good languages, and they have a lot in common. Many people have pointed out that they appear to be converging, feature-wise.

They also have similar problems. Performance is a big one—both of them are too slow, and need compilers and/or VMs. They both also have legacy design decisions they're trying to fix. Ruby's trying to back out of some of its Perl-isms, and Python's still fixing its warts.

What holds you back in Python and Ruby?

SY: Python is wonderfully expressive, but it's also quite prescriptive. Developers hate being told how to do things. For example, there's no reasonable way to do an if/then/else on a single line. Each one of those little things is a rock in your shoe.

For both languages, my biggest concern is concurrency support. After you see what Erlang and Gambit Scheme can do, you quickly conclude that the next big language has to have something like it. But the world's not going to wait around for a perfect solution. We're at a tipping point, and sometime in the next year or two, I think one language will rally enough support to be a phenomenon as big as C++, Perl, and Java were, perfect or not. My money's on Ruby at the moment.

Will Groovy be the next great language?

SY: I don't think so. I was hoping it'd be cool, since among the 10 or 15 halfway-decent JVM languages out there, Groovy seems to have the most hype, and that's important. Technically, it's lacking.

At first glance, Groovy appears to be doing a lot of cool things and making good design decisions. Sadly, it doesn't survive the second glance. The language is a sort of kitchen sink for features, with no coherent vision emerging. The design is more focused on shortcuts than on general expressiveness. There are some good features, but not enough of them.

Except for the marketing, Groovy's execution has been particularly bad. It's still among the slowest JVM languages, and every beta has had obvious showstopper bugs. There's no real documentation, and the language only just got a parser generator after two years. It feels amateurish.

Ruby

Of all the languages generating a buzz in the Java space, Ruby comes up the most frequently. The Java community invests passion in equal parts venom and bliss into the raging Java versus Ruby on Rails debate. This fervor interests me because Ruby, and Rails, get plenty of exposure within the Java community where more mature object-oriented languages like Python and Smalltalk do not. Exposure can translate to more exposure and more users. Developed in 1995, Ruby is relatively mature in calendar years, but it gained popularity first in Japan, and the worldwide community is just now starting to grow. Among the most promising contenders, Ruby has the interesting combination of being relatively mature and simultaneously undiscovered by the Java masses.

In favor

While Ruby doesn't have the support of something like Java, it does have pretty good commercial backing in Japan. It's got a healthy community, and awareness in the Java community. It's also got a good virtual machine. But the beauty of Ruby is primarily in the language. Ruby also tends to solve a few important problems very well:

- Ruby makes metaprogramming feel natural. Reflection is easy, and you can move and change methods quickly. Ruby's modules let you mix in important capabilities without changing any source code.

- Rails, the flagship Ruby framework, makes it easy to build web sites based on relational databases. In the past decade, no other application has been more important.

- Web-based development with other innovative approaches is easy. Ruby has at least three exploratory projects related to continuation servers.

Ruby is extremely dynamic and extensible. You can literally hook into Ruby everywhere. You can replace the methods of a whole class or a single instance at runtime. Ruby developers often introduce methods that themselves introduce other methods and behavior. The net effect is a single hook that lets you add significant capabilities to a class or instance with very little syntax.

In my opinion, metaprogramming in some form will increasingly define modern programming. That's already happening in Java, with persistence engines like Hibernate, programming hooks like interceptors, programming models like aspect-oriented programming, and language extensions like annotations. To do metaprogramming effectively, you need to be able to extend a language to fit seamlessly within a domain. Languages that make this easy will move faster than languages that don't. Java limits the ways that you can extend a class, it makes you work hard to do reflection, and it makes you use unnatural techniques like byte code enhancement, code generation, and dynamic proxies. On the other hand, Ruby handles metaprogramming with ease. For example, the Rails framework, Active

Record, defines belongs_to and has_many methods describing database relationships. Each method adds additional Ruby behavior and attributes to the decorated class. At the most basic level, the Ruby language itself uses metaprogramming to describe attributes. attr_accessor :name is shorthand for this:

```
def name=(value)
  @name=value
end

def name
  @name
end
```

You get a syntax with less repetition, and the language developers did not have to work very hard to give it to you. Of course, Java also does metaprogramming. It just doesn't do it very well.

Ruby interests me for several other reasons, too. Ruby is a chameleon with enough theoretical headroom to grow beyond Rails with ease, and a simple enough syntax to excite beginners and educators. Ruby will let you do functional programming, or play with continuations. You can write full web-based applications, or slip into scripting for rudimentary text processing. Ruby gives you a language that's theoretically pure, and practical.

Ruby might not have the extensive libraries of Java, but it's closing the gap rapidly. It's also worth mentioning that Ruby is doing so with a fraction of the developers, because Ruby is just so productive. As Java moves more and more toward metaprogramming, this productivity gap will increase.

Against

The biggest strike against Ruby right now is the lack of a strong project that lets Ruby run on the JVM. The JRuby project's vision is greater than a simple port to the JVM. So far, the project has had several stops and starts. It's not far enough along to, for example, run Ruby on Rails. Most in the Ruby community don't see the political importance of a language that runs on the JVM, but interest and participation in the project may be picking up. JRuby seeks to let you use Java classes using Ruby idioms. For example, you'll be able to use Ruby code blocks with Java collections. If Microsoft is able to woo the Ruby founders over to .NET's CLR, or if the JRuby project starts picking up momentum, you'll see one of the biggest strikes against Ruby go away. Still, the lack of a credible version that runs on a widely deployed virtual machine, be it Microsoft or Java, is a major strike against Ruby. To be fair, the JRuby project in the months just before publication has made incredible strides. It now passes over 90% of the test cases for the basic

Ruby platform. When it reaches Version 1.0 and can run Ruby on Rails suitably, Ruby will become a much stronger contender. Any language that embraces and extends Java will be in a much stronger political position.

Also, Ruby does not have the excellent commercial backing of some of the other alternatives. For example, Google uses Python extensively. Though Ruby is gaining traction in Japan, and also at places like Amazon.com, it's still a relative unknown. You can't yet hire Ruby programmers in numbers, and your training options are limited. If the Rails project hits a critical mass, that will change in a hurry.

A Word About Lisp

Lisp addicts might wonder why their beloved language is not higher on my list. In fact, Lisp has many of the characteristic of Ruby, with superior metaprogramming, a more extensive language, a good functional model, readable macros, and a clean and consistent interface. Lisp has never had the all-important marketing visionary, a catalyst, or the approachability of Ruby. It's also got history and a reputation to overcome. Ruby also has some other telling advantages: better regular expressions, parallel assignments (x, y = y+1, x+1), effective modules, better encapsulation (like private or protected methods), and standardized threads. True, many of these things have been done in Lisp, but Ruby provides a clean, standard solution in the language.

Overall

Major factors, including a comparative lack of libraries and the absence of a credible JVM implementation, argue against Ruby, but it's still a primary contender because of a possible catalyst in Rails, economic justification in productivity, and the database and web libraries that make it practical for a good set of problems in the enterprise. The language is theoretically pure and strong enough to last. You can integrate Java applications through web services and communication protocols, or C applications through a native interface. It has a virtual machine, and dialects for all major operating systems. If something challenges Java soon, I think Ruby is the most likely candidate.

Python

If ever you are looking for a test case for the requirement of a catalyst, look no further than Python. It has just about everything we're looking for—a good metamodel, a clean and readable syntax, dynamic typing, flexibility, and power. Python is also pretty natural for Java programmers. Here's a Python example from python.org:

```
def invert(table):
    index = { }                # empty dictionary
    for key in table.keys( ):
        value = table[key]
        if not index.has_key(value):
            index[value] = [ ] # empty list
        index[value].append(key)
    return index
```

You'll notice a couple of striking things about Python right off the bat. First, unlike Java, you don't have to have a full class definition. Python is equally at home as a procedural language or an object-oriented one. Second, you don't see any syntax to end a block of code because whitespace matters. Indentation determines code grouping. Like many great programming languages, Python holds appeal for both beginners and advanced programmers. There's much to like.

In favor

Python has many of the same advantages as Ruby. It's dynamically typed, object-oriented, concise, and friendlier to applications than Java. It's easy to read, very consistent, and free. You can find interesting free libraries to do everything from web development to ORM. Python has the advantages of a productive applications language, and relatively numerous libraries. You can run it on Java's virtual machine in an environment called Jython.

Python has an extensive vibrant community. You can find support, hire developers, and get consulting. The open source libraries are numerous, but nowhere near the extent of Java's. Though overall growth has been sporadic, Python has gained limited traction in spots, in flagship accounts like Google.

Against

While Python has a few good web development frameworks, it doesn't yet have a Java-killer like Rails. I'm already seeing a few Rails clones emerge, like Subway (*http://subway.python-hosting.com/*), but none of them has the marketing punch behind Ruby on Rails. In fact, the primary strike against

Python is the lack of a catalyst of any kind. The Python community is full of technical vision, but the marketing vision has so far been lacking.

Several influential Python bloggers have recognized the Ruby buzz in the Java community, and they make the point that Python doesn't yet have that compelling framework that might convert a Java developer. Java consultant Stuart Halloway moved to Python for better productivity, but he believes the Python community does not actively court the Java community. Many of them believe that Java is irrelevant.

A few minor technical details hold back Python. Some don't like the idea that whitespace is significant. That turns off some Java developers who like to condense repetitive Java constructs, such as default constructors or accessors, like this:

```
public String getName( ) {return name;}
public void setName(String name) {this.name=name;}
```

Overzealous enforcement of anything leads to problems with programmers, and whitespace is no different. When you dogmatically enforce whitespace, you also limit your expressiveness. For example, you might type:

```
if ( character == eol ) { line=file.next( ); count ++; }
```

because it expresses a single coherent thought as a sentence. Whitespace alone isn't the problem; it's the dogmatic enforcement of endless subjects like this one that rub some developers the wrong way. The overriding Python philosophy says there should be one obvious way to do something, and the language designers often go to great lengths to maintain those conventions, sometimes sacrificing flexibility to do so. The hope is that consistency will override any disadvantages. In the past, these kinds of attitudes have limited the flexibility of a language. Unless the language designers have perfect imagination, it's often best to let a language evolve in several different ways at once. The Python leadership does have a reputation as being somewhat frosty and dogmatic on these types of issues.

You can do metaprogramming in Python, with method or function pointers and using reflection, as well as other techniques. Those that have experience in both Python and Ruby seem to think that metaprogramming is more natural in Ruby. You can work with objects or not, which is a double-edged sword. Some (like the founder of Ruby) say Python might not be object-oriented enough.

Overall

Python has most of the tangible benefits you'd expect in a dynamic language, but it lacks the intangibles. New languages either pop when they're discovered, or they don't pop at all. Python never popped at all. Python is a nonentity in the Java community. That's a shame, because Jython makes it a viable political option when languages like Ruby aren't even considered. Python proponents looking to displace Java can argue that using Python amounts to a different syntax and some different libraries, and the rest of the infrastructure remains unchanged, but the often negative Java sentiment within the Python community works against Jython. Most Python developers don't understand that Java, too, is a powerful language, based on its extensive community, which leads to more libraries and massive commercial support.

With the emergence of some kind of killer app, Python could well emerge as a Java killer. Without it, Java developers think they already know what they need to know about Python, so there's no real reason to give it a second look.

Groovy

Groovy is a new dynamic scripting language. It's built to run in the JVM. It's backed with the JCP with a JSR. It's still young, and it seems to be having problems getting to a solid, stable release.

Groovy is particularly interesting because it has none of the fundamental problems with marketing and acceptance in the Java community that the other languages have. Groovy's problem has been the execution: the speed and the implementation. So far, Groovy has lacked the sound, technical underpinnings of the other languages in this chapter, as well as a visionary to both innovate and see inventions through to a sound, stable conclusion.

In favor

I want to like Groovy. I really do. It has the marketing support, hype, and attention in the Java community. It runs in the virtual machine, ties in well to the Java language, and has political backing from Sun. James Strachan, a hero of sorts within the Java community, is the primary father, bringing an instant fanfare and credibility to the project. With a formal JSR, it's usually easier to introduce Groovy into a company as a scripting language than some other dynamic language. The syntax, though inconsistent, is terse, and the Groovy JSR supports many of the important features that dynamic languages should, at least in letter.

Against

The problem is that Groovy is just so hard to like. To this point, Groovy has been quirky, unpredictable, and full of bugs. Many features, introduced in very early versions of Groovy, remain uncompleted, and early shortcuts led to an unsound grammar. Early versions of Groovy used a hand-generated parser rather than a parser generator, such as ANTLR. After the syntax was belatedly retrofitted to ANTLR, the syntax was set in many ways, and the grammar was unwieldy.

Today, the fledgling language continues to struggle. People leading the project seem to be more interested with introducing new ideas than finishing old ones. Blogger Mike Spille was a Groovy insider who worked on the language, and later abandoned it due to significant problems with the language, technical vision, and stability. He pointed out major holes in the language and syntax around closures (a kind of code block) here: *http://www.pyrasun.com/mike/mt/archives/2005/01/13/21.56.41/index.html.* You can also see a later heated debate between two of the early Groovy contributors on TheServerSide.com here: *http://www.theserverside.com/news/thread.tss?thread_id=33157.*

It seems like each major beta release breaks existing Groovy applications. Worse, the first major Groovy specification request broke existing applications. That's not good. Many of the core Groovy developers also seem to be leaving the original JSR team.

Overall

With a formal JSR backing it, Groovy is politically in a good place to succeed. After all, you could argue that EJB succeeded based on the reputations of the supporters, despite significant technical limitations. Groovy has some energy and hype, but a few false starts seem to be stalling the momentum. I'll undoubtedly get flamed for saying so, but right now, Groovy is much too young and too unstable to deserve serious consideration for any production application, let alone standardization.

That Groovy is buggy and unstable as a beta doesn't trouble me so much, though you'd expect core language features and syntax to be set very early, but basic features like closures don't work. I'm most concerned with the overall process. The community process standardized the Groovy language before it was mature, or even stabilized. To move forward in a productive way, Groovy must first solidify the major feature set, then recover some lost momentum, and then prove itself in some commercial niche before it will be considered as a significant candidate to replace Java anywhere. Until then, it's merely an experiment. I hope it succeeds, but I don't think it will. It simply has too far to go.

.NET

.NET is the only nonprogramming language that I've mentioned as a credible successor to Java. .NET is Microsoft's latest development platform, deserving special mention because it has a massive library, and a language-agnostic engine called the Common Language Runtime (CLR) that sits on top. If Microsoft makes .NET successful, and truly language-neutral, it could serve as a launching pad of sorts for many languages. Right now, like the JVM, the CLR has some technical issues to overcome before it can fully support dynamic languages like Ruby, but Microsoft is committed to doing so.

Language options

At some level, the programming libraries underneath .NET are far more important than the language. Their usage models frequently dictate application structure, often more than the choice of programming language. Still, Microsoft offers several programming languages, targeted at vastly different communities.

Visual Basic for .NET

Microsoft has a real problem on its hands with Visual Basic programmers. It seems many of those hundreds of thousands of active developers just don't like .NET, and they're looking for alternatives. The .NET framework changed the programming model for Visual Basic. So far, most of them either are actively deciding to pursue alternatives, or are passively waiting to upgrade. Either way, Microsoft loses. As a result, it looks like Visual Basic is in trouble.

In public, Java and .NET developers don't mix, but each community often reluctantly admits the strengths of the other. While married to a platform, Java developers have often stolen secretive longing looks at Visual Basic's productivity and user interface development framework. Visual Basic users secretly returned the flirtations, admiring Java's structure, if not productivity. I'm making an educated guess that Microsoft thought it could sneak in some more structure, believing that the BASIC syntax would trump the unfamiliar frameworks underneath. They were wrong.

Microsoft is making some moves toward satisfying the Visual Basic community. Some plans seem to favor a Visual Basic classic edition, which looks and acts more like the Visual Basic of old. To me, that move smacks of new Coke and Coca-Cola Classic, a public relations disaster.

C#

C# (pronounced *see sharp*) is a programming language that fills the role of Java for the .NET platform. There's not much to say about C# in a book called *Beyond Java*, because it's built to be similar to Java. You'll see a few minor exceptions, like reliance on unchecked exceptions rather than checked exceptions, and some syntactic sugar. Many of the recent changes in Java, like annotations and autoboxing, were introduced to keep up with . NET. For the most part, though, those looking to trade in Java and simultaneously lose their problems will find a whole new stack of problems, with a similar size and shape. C# is merely Java's evil twin.

Still, Microsoft seems willing to separate old versions of C# to a new language, under development, called C Omega. This language would potentially make some significant strides forward, and possibly even break compatibility with C#. Such a language could potentially offer the features of much more dynamic languages, with the commercial backing of Microsoft, and the CLR as a portable virtual machine. It bears watching. Still, it's proprietary, and many won't give it a serious try for that reason alone.

Other languages on the CLR

What's intriguing about .NET is not the Microsoft languages. It's the promise of open source languages on the CLR. Right now, since most of Microsoft's energy is undoubtedly focused on Visual Basic, C++, and C#, you're not going to see a library that's built to take advantage of important concepts like code blocks and continuations. Still, Microsoft actively courts insiders in the Ruby and Python communities, so you could see credible implementations of those languages soon.

A weakness and a strength

.NET and the CLR have one major problem: Microsoft. Sometimes its weight and muscle work in your favor, and sometimes they don't. It's not likely that the CLR will ever run as well on other platforms as it does on, say, Linux. With Microsoft's heavily proprietary stance and a complete lack of portability, it's tough to see the Java community embracing .NET. You may be surprised that I don't think Microsoft's posture will remain so pervasively proprietary, especially on the server side.

I've said before that market leaders want to be proprietary. All others need open standards to compete. Microsoft is simultaneously the market leader for client-side operating systems, and lumped in with everyone else (or with Internet and Enterprise development). Proprietary frameworks make sense on the client, where Microsoft has had a near-monopoly for a long time now. They make a little less sense on the server side, where they've been unable to crack the market for medium and large systems. In time, I believe that Microsoft will recognize this reality and jump on the open source software bandwagon. I'm not the only one who thinks so. I sit on the expert panel of NoFluffJustStuff, one of the most successful and influential Java conferences outside of JavaOne. Stuart Halloway, one of the most respected Java consultants in areas such as metaprogramming and reflection, feels strongly that Microsoft will be the biggest open source vendor in the world, and Dave Thomas seems to agree.

If Microsoft does happen to move toward open source software in a credible way, and the Java community recognizes this, Microsoft will open the door to Java on the CLR, and more importantly, to the languages beyond.

Minor Contenders

Now, it's time to put on an asbestos suit and my +4 plate mail. I debated whether to include any sections on Perl, Lisp, PHP, or Smalltalk. They're fantastic languages in their own right. I just don't think they're next.

If you're deeply religious about any of these languages, you can just read these one-sentence summaries, and skip to the next section: *Perl's too loose and too messy, PHP is too close to the HTML, Lisp is not accessible, and Smalltalk wasn't Java.*

If you already feel slighted and you must read on—if you're a language cultist and I've mentioned your pet language in also-rans, or worse, didn't mention your pet language at all—go ahead and fire up your Gmail client and your thesaurus, and drop me a nasty note. Ted Neward reviewed this book, so I can take a few more euphemisms for the word *sucks*. Just keep this in mind: I'm not saying that your language isn't good, or popular. I'm just saying 10 years from now, we probably won't look back at any of these languages as the Java killer.

Steve Yegge: Perl, Lisp, PHP, and Smalltalk

Why won't Perl replace Java?   **SY:**   Well, I'd say Perl was pretty darn successful, and it's still one of the most popular languages around. Perl had world-class marketing: Larry Wall understands programmers, and he's funny and articulate. Perl filled a desperate niche in the Unix-scripting world, and another with CGI. Perl was successful because it was executed superbly, just as Java was.

I do think it's on the wane, though. Perl used to be more productive than the alternatives, so you could argue it was ugly all you wanted, but people got their jobs done faster. But newer languages, Ruby in particular, are changing the game.

Perl is the all-time king of pointless abstractions, like references and typeglobs, one-off shortcuts, and plain old gross hacks, with extra syntax sprayed on to cover the smell. It was productive, but programmers will take the path of least resistance, and Ruby offers orders of magnitude less friction.

What about Lisp?   **SY:**   That's a tough one. Lisp has world-class survival skills. People keep reinventing or rediscovering it, but Lisp is also a family of families of mutually incompatible designs and implementations, and *none* of the existing ones looks like a sure winner. For example, Common Lisp needs an overhaul, but redesign by committee is exactly the wrong thing for CL at this point. Lisp needs a benevolent dictator with good instincts, great execution, and great marketing.

And PHP?   **SY:**   PHP's very popular, and getting more so, because it makes web programming easier than most of the alternatives, but Ruby on Rails is going to change all that. There *will* be a simplification pass to web programming at some point. PHP's not driving a simplification pass of the Web. It just tries to help you cope with the existing complexity. The language is heavily weighed down by its Perl legacy, with lots of confusing and regrettable design decisions. And it's not in the same league as more powerful languages like Ruby, Python, and Lisp.

Is Smalltalk next?

SY: I doubt it. In the end, languages have to have buzz and momentum, and I just don't see any marketing for Smalltalk. The community got the wind knocked out of it by Java, and it doesn't seem to have ever recovered.

PHP

PHP is an open source scripting language that's been gathering momentum since the early 2000s. It's a markup language that's designed to be embedded into HTML. It's very easy to quickly develop simple web applications in PHP, but those applications typically have little back-end structure. For these reasons, it's not really targeting the same niche as Java applications, though it's sometimes been pressed into service in much the same way. Here is "Hello, World" in PHP:

```
<html>
  <head>
    <title>Hello, World</title>
  </head>
  <body>
    <?php echo '<p>Hello World</p>'; ?>
  </body>
</html>
```

Web programmers recognize this as an HTML scripting language. The code is processed on the server side, so pure HTML can be sent down to the client. It actually handles this kind of scripting pretty well, but it's purely a tag language. PHP's problem is the structure behind the view. It's possible to use PHP for layers behind the view, but it's awkward and cumbersome in that role.

PHP is going to make some serious noise as a pure web-based scripting language, though. In one of the strangest moves in 2005, IBM announced support for PHP. This move undoubtedly targeted the small and medium-size businesses that tend to embrace PHP. IBM can now theoretically sell them software and services to round out their implementations. PHP seems to be a natural language for those Visual Basic users who don't want to make the move to .NET. Like Visual Basic, it will be pressed into service in places where it doesn't fit as developers search for simplicity in the wrong places.

With the most basic Google skills, you can find dozens of papers that attempt to compare Java and PHP. You'll tend to find two types of comments. The PHP camp says that Java isn't productive enough, and the Java camp says that PHP isn't structured enough. I tend to agree with both of them. The primary danger with PHP for small applications is that they can grow into big PHP applications, and you're left without the structure that will let you easily maintain and extend your web applications.

Perl

Perl is a very popular language for programmers who look for raw first-cut efficiency. Perl was quite popular for shell scripts, before simpler alternatives were available. In terms of productivity, Perl has many of the characteristics of other highly productive languages. It's very expressive, terse, and dynamically typed. It gives you freedom to do what you want to do, and has a rapid feedback loop. Paul Graham calls it a great language for "hacking," or rapid experimental programming. Much of the Internet is powered by CGI Perl scripts.

Perl does have a downside. When you look at overall productivity of a language, you've also got to take things like maintenance and readability into account. Perl tends to rate very poorly among experts on a readability scale. As with Java, much of Perl's problem is cultural. Some Perl programmers would rather chop off their little finger than type four extra characters, whether the characters improve readability or not. After all, programs that were hard to *write* should be hard to *read*. Other Perl problems relate to the language itself. Perl's object orientation is obviously bolted on, and Perl has a secret handshake of sorts, in the form of many cryptic syntactic shortcuts that only the mother of Perl could love. A whole lot of us at one time or another have had some sort of love/hate relationship with Perl. It's interesting to talk about, but it's pretty much the antithesis of Java, and it's likely not going to make a dent.

Smalltalk

Smalltalk is a beautiful language invented way before its time. Smalltalk and Lisp are probably the two languages that share the most with Ruby. Smart developers used Smalltalk to build successful object-oriented applications long before Java was even a twinkle in Gossling's eye. And not-so-smart developers used Smalltalk to build some of the ugliest object-oriented code ever written. In truth, for the most part, in the mid- and late 1970s, we just didn't have the wisdom or the processing power for OOP yet, and we didn't have features like just-in-time compilers.

In Chapter 8, you saw the elegance of the Smalltalk language. It's object-oriented through and through, and the syntax is remarkably consistent. Smalltalk's syntax probably seemed strange to the masses of programmers who grew up coding COBOL, BASIC, Pascal, C, or C++. Most of the businesses I know of that actually tried Smalltalk were able to get their applications out in time, they just never were able to integrate those applications with the rest of the world.

Smalltalk never was able to lure C and C++ developers away, because it was too alien and had the perception of being too slow. As the small Smalltalk community waited for objects to emerge, Java's founders aggressively grabbed the C++ community by the throat, forced it to come along with C++ syntax and usage models, and offered solutions to solve the most pressing problems the C developers encountered. As we showed, Java was effectively a compromise between perfect OO and the C++ community. Later, IBM made a move to buy OTI, a maker of Smalltalk virtual machines. In one last push for Smalltalk, IBM built a common virtual machine into an IDE called Visual Age with the hopes that the common JVM could lend credibility to Smalltalk. It was too little, too late. We were too content in our newfound freedom, safely and freshly away from all things C++, in the arms of Java.

It's hard to imagine Smalltalk rising up from 30 years of obscurity to dominate. It's probably not going to happen. Still, you can find a small but active community of Smalltalk developers. Disney built Squeak, a Smalltalk dialect and implementation focusing on multimedia. A handful of other dialects are also still around.

In the end, Smalltalk may yet make an impact on development, but as the proving ground for ideas like continuation servers. You'll find evidence of Smalltalk's object model and syntax everywhere. Most notably, Ruby liberally borrows code blocks and idioms like returning self. I think continuation servers will ultimately play a role in web development. They just make too much sense, are too natural, and are too compelling. Smalltalk is where all the continuation research is happening.

Lisp

Lisp is an extremely powerful language that excels in its strange but pure syntax, abstract modeling, and raw efficiency. In Lisp, everything is a list, including Lisp programs. Metaprogramming in Lisp feels natural, and is quite popular. Important ideas like aspect-oriented programming and continuation servers started in Lisp. Several dialects like Dylan and Scheme appear periodically, but none has achieved much success in the commercial mainstream, beyond a macro language for the Emacs. Still, start-ups often use Lisp because once you learn it, you can be incredibly productive. Some very successful programmers like Paul Graham (author of *Hackers & Painters*) believe Lisp is the most expressive programming language, and they could be right.

Lisp's community has always been made up of intelligent developers, and it's still popular among academics. In fact, some of the best programming universities, like MIT, emphasize Lisp early, to get students to quickly think in the abstract, and to expose them to functional techniques.

Maybe all languages will once again return to Lisp, but I don't think that Lisp itself is the ultimate answer. It's just too alien, and it takes too much time and effort to learn.

Functional Languages

It's probably a bit too early to be talking about functional languages, because we seem to be moving toward object-oriented languages instead. Still, functional programming provides a higher abstraction and very good productivity. It's possible that some functional language could explode, with the right killer app.

Haskell and Erlang are two of a family of programming languages called functional languages. Functions are the focus of functional languages. I use the word *function* in the pure mathematical sense:

- Functions have no side effects. This oddity takes some getting used to for most procedural programmers, but also has significant benefits.
- Functions return values.
- You can use the return value of a function anywhere you can use the returned type.

You can do functional programming in languages like Ruby and Lisp, but for research or purity, often it's better to use a purer language. Here's a Haskell example, which computes the factorial of a number:

```
fact 0 = 1
fact n = n * fact (n - 1)
```

Then, as expected, you can compute the value like this:

```
fact 10
```

Here's a Fibonacci sequence (where each number is the sum of the previous two):

```
fib 0 = 0
fib 1 = 1
fib n = fib (n-1) + fib (n-2)
```

Functional languages let you work at a higher level of abstraction. Haskell has good traction in research and academic communities, and seems to be gaining a small, vibrant commercial community. It's easy to teach, and as such, it could provide a doorway into functional programming, much like Pascal provided a doorway to procedural languages.

You can see the power of functional programming in the Erlang language. Developed at Ericsson, Erlang's main focus is concurrency. Erlang lets you easily create and use threads, and communicate between them. Erlang also improves distributed computing, because the location of threads is transparent—a thread might be in the same process as another, or on a different machine. It's productive, dynamically typed, garbage collected, and very small. There's been a recent spike of interest in Erlang for applications that need excellent support for concurrency and distribution. It's used in production at some high-profile sites. At this point, Erlang is still in its infancy as a general-purpose language. Users tend to use it in conjunction with C (for better performance), and it doesn't have any real user interface library. Still, Erlang is powerful in its niche, and it could make an impact in the intermediate future, directly or as a derivative.

The Next Big Thing

Of course, the whole premise of this book is arrogant beyond belief. I'm making an incredible number of assumptions and drawing some aggressive conclusions based on little more than a couple of dozen interviews, a keen sense of intuition, and a few massive piles of circumstantial evidence.

Java may need nothing more than a little overhaul. Maybe the problem is in the massively complex libraries, and a few rewrites with some tweaks of the language would extend Java's leadership for 10 more years. Maybe the community's culture doesn't help define our libraries. The driving vendors may do an about-face and focus more on simplifying the 80% path instead of building yet another XML-obsessed framework. The JCP could suddenly start supporting the best existing frameworks based on experience instead of standardizing a good idea that was born in a committee.

Maybe Dion Almaer is right, and the big companies that drive this industry are not remotely interested in moving away from Java, and we'll all be saddled with Java for the foreseeable future.

Maybe Jason Hunter is right, and the next big thing won't be a programming language at all. Maybe Java's all we'll ever need, and we'll use that foundation to move up the abstraction ladder. Maybe Glenn and David are both right and there won't be one next big thing, but lots of next little things, and both metaprogramming and continuations will play a significant role.

I don't know the ultimate answers, so I've leaned on my mentors and peers. The interviews in this book are the opinions of some of the people I respect the most. It's been an honor to share these few pages with them. I'm not ready to say that Java's dead, or that Ruby is next, or that continuation servers will reign supreme. I just know:

- I'm hurting right now, and my customers are, too. It's getting harder and harder to teach my customers to satisfy themselves with Java.

- Certain things, like baby-sitting a relational database with a web-based UI, should be easier in Java, after nearly 10 years of effort, but they're still cumbersome.

- The same people that dozed in conversations about other languages two years ago seem to be paying attention now. My "Beyond Java" talks, at Java conferences, are continually packed.

As for me, my eyes are wide open. I've seen what the alternatives can do. In particular, Ruby on Rails lets me build reliable code fast, and put it in front of my customer with more confidence and frequency. I didn't actively seek an alternative—on the contrary, with four Java books out and a reputation in the Java space, I've got every reason to maintain the status quo. I did find that some of the alternatives are compelling, and make for a smooth transition.

A Charge to You

If you're a Java developer and this message is troubling you, that's natural. You've got good reasons to feel threatened with this challenge of your world view. You may feel even more unsettled when someone challenges the foundation of your livelihood. I'd encourage you to put this book down and do some research of your own.

Look around. When James Duncan Davidson did, he found a language that responded to his needs for low-level user interface development. Stuart Halloway found a language that let his start-up move at the speed of his ideas. Dave Thomas found the foundation for an increasingly important publishing series. Glenn Vanderburg found languages friendlier to his beloved metaprogramming techniques.

If you decide to expand your horizons beyond Java, you may find that I'm right, and some of the alternatives I've explored here, or even some I didn't, unleash you. You'll be surfing the next wave that propels us forward.

If I'm wrong, Java will still be there for you; heck, even COBOL is still there for you. But to you, it won't be the same Java. Other languages will expand your horizons to other approaches, just as a wave of Java developers will bring our unique view of the world with us. If you spend some time in Smalltalk, you'll probably use Java's reflection more, you'll look for more opportunities to invert control by simulating code blocks, and you may well tone down your use of XML. (OK, I may have pushed things too far with that one.) If you explore continuation servers, you may look for a way to simulate that programming style in Java. If you explore Rails, you'll likely learn to pay more attention to defaults and convention. Hibernate, Spring, Struts, servlets, collections, and the JDO could all use these techniques.

Pick up your eyes by learning a language. Expand your mind to something a little more powerful, and a lot more dynamic. Warp your perspective to functional programming or continuations. Annoy your friends with a contrarian's view. Tell them that you don't think the world's flat. There's a whole universe out there, beyond Java.

Index

We'd like to hear your suggestions for improving our indexes. Send email to *index@oreilly.com*.

unnatural stretching, 7
vendor support, 44
Java 1.5, 64
Java 5, 8
Java Server Faces (JSF), 70
Java Server Pages (JSP), 41
Java Specification Request (JSR), 8
Java Virtual Machine (JVM), 35
portability and, 35
Java Virtual machine (JVM), 8, 81
JavaScript, 25, 41, 76
JBoss, 45, 109
JDBC, 79
JDO, 53
JMX, 65
JRuby, 38, 76
JUnit, 45, 54
Jython, 38

K

kayaking, as a metaphor for
programming, 1
killer app
catalyst for new language, 84
PHP applications, 84
Ruby metaprogramming
environments, 84
Smalltalk continuation servers, 84
King, Gavin, 69

L

languages, functional, 176
languages that could supplant
Java, 73–94
learning curve, 52
legacy requirements, 78
libraries, 52, 71
limitations, 55
of Java, 4
Lisp, 73, 164, 172
pros and cons, 176
Lotus 1-2-3 spreadsheet, as killer
app, 84
Lucene, 45

M

marketing the new language, 81
Matsumoto, Yukihiro (Matz), 91

memory-stompers, 17
metaprogramming, 10, 11, 162, 176
and the killer app question, 137
method interception, 109
Microsoft
influences on application
development, 15
Windows, security and, 37
middleware, 44, 51
mixin, 20
mixins, 108
mobile applications, 39
model-view-controller (MVC)
frameworks, 7, 41
modules, 108
multiple inheritance, 20

N

navigation and flow, 141
nested includes, 18
.NET
Java versus, 47
pros and cons, 169
Netscape Navigator, 23
Neward, Ted (interview), 64

O

object orientation requirement, 89
Object Relational Mapping (ORM), 4,
53, 79
object-oriented programming
(OOP), 16
open source community, 29
open source software, 81, 82
future of Java and, 68
IBM and, 45
importance of, 45
open source tools and Java, 6
overloading, 64
owls and ostriches, 1–12

P

perceptions, changing, 159
performance, 122
Perl, 15, 69, 73, 82, 172
potential replacement for Java, 90
pros and cons, 174
persistence frameworks, 7

About the Author

Bruce A. Tate is a kayaker, mountain biker, father, author, and Java programmer in Austin, Texas. His five books include the Jolt award-winning *Better, Faster, Lighter Java* (O'Reilly) and the bestselling *Bitter Java* (Manning). His 17 years of experience include stints at IBM, two failed start-ups, and his own independent consulting practice, called J2Life, LLC.

Colophon

Our look is the result of reader comments, our own experimentation, and feedback from distribution channels. Distinctive covers complement our distinctive approach to technical topics, breathing personality and life into potentially dry subjects.

The animal on the cover of *Beyond Java* is a bassaris. The bassaris (*Bassaris astuta*) is a North American carnivore found in Mexico, Texas, and California. About the size of a typical domestic cat, the bassaris is closely related to the raccoon and fox.

This brown- or tan-furred animal has a black-and-white-ringed tail that grows as long as the length of its body. The size of the tail provides balance for negotiating narrow ledges and limbs, and even allowsthe animal to reverse direction by performing a cartwheel. It can rotate its hind feet 180 degrees, giving it the ability to rapidly descend cliffs or trees, as well as cacti.

The bassaris is a nocturnal, non-aggressive creature. It lives in caves, crevices, and hollow trees, and has been found in abandoned buildings and even attics of occupied dwellings. It has been known to visit campsites and rummage through gear, sometimes taking items—especially shiny ones. An agile climber, it negotiates trees and sheer rock faces with ease.

Foraging mainly at night on small birds, rodents, lizards, snakes, invertebrates, and fruit, the bassaris will also regularly consume carrion. Fruit is a main component of its diet, and this may reduce its need for water.

Trapped for fur in some locations, the bassaris is also frequently tamed as a pet, especially in parts of Mexico. It is called by several different names, including the mountain cat, civit cat, and cat squirrel. The Mexican name for this creature is *cacomixl*. Its scientific name (*bassaris*) stems from the Greek word for fox, and in some Greek mythological tales, Dionysus wears a bassaris, which symbolizes new life.

Darren Kelly was the production editor, and Audrey Doyle was the copyeditor for *Beyond Java*. Sada Preisch proofread the book. Matt Hutchinson and Claire Cloutier provided quality control. Reg Aubry wrote the index.

Ellie Volckhausen designed the cover of this book, based on a series design by Edie Freedman. The cover image is a 19th-century engraving from *Johnson's Natural History*. Karen Montgomery produced the cover layout with Adobe InDesign CS using Adobe's ITC Garamond font.

David Futato designed the interior layout. This book was converted by Joe Wizda to FrameMaker 5.5.6 with a format conversion tool created by Erik Ray, Jason McIntosh, Neil Walls, and Mike Sierra that uses Perl and XML technologies. The text font is Linotype Birka; the heading font is Adobe Myriad Condensed; and the code font is LucasFont's TheSans Mono Condensed. The illustrations that appear in the book were produced by Robert Romano, Jessamyn Read, and Lesley Borash using Macromedia FreeHand MX and Adobe Photoshop CS. This colophon was written by Darren Kelly.

Better than e-books

Buy *Beyond Java* and access the digital edition FREE on Safari for 45 days.

Go to www.oreilly.com/go/safarienabled
and type in coupon code FXAQ-38MC-FWEY-UUCD-H5CR

Search
thousands of
top tech books

Download
whole chapters

Cut and Paste
code examples

Find
answers fast

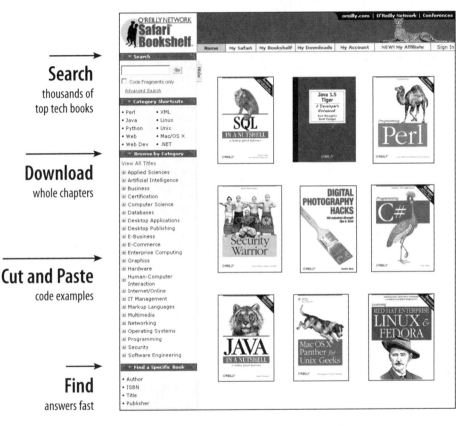

Search Safari! The premier electronic reference
library for programmers and IT professionals.

Related Titles from O'Reilly

Java

Ant: The Definitive Guide,
  2nd Edition

Better, Faster, Lighter Java

Beyond Java

Eclipse

Eclipse Cookbook

Eclipse IDE Pocket Guide

Enterprise JavaBeans,
  4th Edition

Hardcore Java

Head First Design Patterns

Head First Design Patterns
  Poster

Head First Java

Head First Servlets & JSP

Head First EJB

Hibernate:
  A Developer's Notebook

J2EE Design Patterns

Java 1.5 Tiger:
  A Developer's Notebook

Java & XML Data Binding

Java & XML

Java Cookbook, *2nd Edition*

Java Data Objects

Java Database Best Practices

Java Enterprise Best Practices

Java Enterprise in a Nutshell,
  3nd Edition

Java Examples in a Nutshell,
  3rd Edition

Java Extreme Programming
  Cookbook

Java in a Nutshell, *5th Edition*

Java Management Extensions

Java Message Service

Java Network Programming,
  2nd Edition

Java NIO

Java Performance Tuning,
  2nd Edition

Java RMI

Java Security, *2nd Edition*

JavaServer Faces

Java ServerPages,
  2nd Edition

Java Servlet & JSP
  Cookbook

Java Servlet Programming,
  2nd Edition

Java Swing, *2nd Edition*

Java Web Services in a
  Nutshell

JBoss:
  A Developer's Notebook

Learning Java, *2nd Edition*

Mac OS X for Java Geeks

Maven:
  A Developer's Notebook

Programming Jakarta Struts,
  2nd Edition

QuickTime for Java:
  A Developer's Notebook

Spring:
  A Developer's Notebook

Swing Hacks

Tomcat:
  The Definitive Guide

WebLogic:
  The Definitive Guide

Keep in touch with O'Reilly

Download examples from our books

To find example files from a book, go to:
www.oreilly.com/catalog select the book,
and follow the "Examples" link.

Register your O'Reilly books

Register your book at *register.oreilly.com*
Why register your books? Once you've
registered your O'Reilly books you can:

- Win O'Reilly books, T-shirts or discount
  coupons in our monthly drawing.

- Get special offers available only to
  registered O'Reilly customers.

- Get catalogs announcing new books
  (US and UK only).

- Get email notification of new editions
  of the O'Reilly books you own.

Join our email lists

Sign up to get topic-specific email announce-
ments of new books and conferences, special
offers, and O'Reilly Network technology
newsletters at:

elists.oreilly.com

It's easy to customize your free elists subscription so you'll get exactly the O'Reilly
news you want.

Get the latest news, tips, and tools

www.oreilly.com

- "Top 100 Sites on the Web"—PC Magazine
- CIO Magazine's Web Business 50 Awards

Our web site contains a library of comprehensive product information (including book
excerpts and tables of contents), download-
able software, background articles, interviews
with technology leaders, links to relevant
sites, book cover art, and more.

Work for O'Reilly

Check out our web site for current
employment opportunities:

jobs.oreilly.com

Contact us

O'Reilly Media, Inc.
1005 Gravenstein Hwy North
Sebastopol, CA 95472 USA
Tel: 707-827-7000 or 800-998-9938
 (6am to 5pm PST)
Fax: 707-829-0104

Contact us by email

For answers to problems regarding
your order or our products:
order@oreilly.com

To request a copy of our latest catalog:
catalog@oreilly.com

For book content technical questions
or corrections: **booktech@oreilly.com**

For educational, library, government,
and corporate sales: **corporate@oreilly.com**

To submit new book proposals to our
editors and product managers:
proposals@oreilly.com

For information about our international
distributors or translation queries:
international@oreilly.com

For information about academic
use of O'Reilly books:
adoption@oreilly.com
or visit:
academic.oreilly.com

For a list of our distributors outside
of North America check out:
international.oreilly.com/distributors.html

Order a book online

www.oreilly.com/order_new

Our books are available at most retail and online bookstores.
To order direct: 1-800-998-9938 • *order@oreilly.com* • *www.oreilly.com*
Online editions of most O'Reilly titles are available by subscription at *safari.oreilly.com*